ENDORSEM

MW01137198

"Leap Beyond AI" is a must-read for leaders navigating the intersection of technology and humanity in the AI era. Micheline Nader masterfully blends visionary concepts with practical strategies in a framework that empowers leaders to embrace disruption, align wellness, and leverage AI ethically while preserving human qualities. With exercises and actionable guidance, this book not only inspires a new generation of leaders to adapt, innovate, and thrive, it's a call to evolve with purpose and compassion."

Hisham Hamadeh
- Senior Vice President,
Global Head of Data Science & AI, Genmab
- Wharton School of Business, Princeton,
New Jersey, United States

"Micheline's latest book focuses beautifully on the critical role of human leadership in the age of AI. She so eloquently articulates the value of human empathy, intellect, decision making and communication in the age of machine learning and artificial intelligence. Her framing of this new horizon as a "new beginning" rather than an end for human leaders is a critically important message at this time, as innovation and disruption become the new normal. This book is a must read for anyone who wants to understand the role that we will play in shaping the future intersection between "man" and "machine"."

Michael J. Avaltroni, Ph.D.
- President of Fairleigh Dickinson University

"Today's Executive Leaders are experiencing a challenging paradigm shift on how AI will impact their organizations.

Grounded in her well-established LEAP Principles, Micheline lays out the compelling case for leaders to embrace how AI can partner with these Principals and positively impact their organization.

Full of practical leadership exercises, this work serves as a playbook on how to think about what AI is and is not today, and what it will become.

Rising above the chatter on this subject, LEAP Beyond AI is essential reading for leaders who need to understand and implement this rapidly evolving technology while remaining 'human'."

Stephen F. Bozer
- Senior Vice President, Human Health, Flavine North America, Inc.

"Wither the leader in the age of AI? It's a question that Micheline Nader tackles with great verve and conviction in her third book on leadership, Leap Beyond AI! As we prepare to LEAP forward into the technofuture, Nader is quite empathic that leadership will matter even more and underscores the need for leaders to bridge the dichotomy often portrayed between human intelligence and artificial intelligence. She transports the reader over the evolving landscape where AI is becoming increasingly embedded in our daily life. She then offers a very practical toolkit for how current and aspiring leaders can continue to harness this power and impact their organization performance. Leap Beyond AI provides an essential roadmap for the leader intending to guide their organization on a path to sustainable success!"

James Almeida
- Dean, Silberman College of Business, FDU

"As an AI researcher, I'm often asked about the future of work and the role of leaders. 'LEAP Beyond AI' provides the most insightful and practical guidance I've seen on how leaders can effectively integrate AI while retaining the core human elements of leadership. Nader's LEAP process gives an actionable framework for leaders to not only survive, but thrive, in the age of AI. Her focus on consciousness and ethical considerations is especially vital."

James Barrood
- Founder/CEO, Innovation+ | INNOVATE100
- Advisor, Tech Council Ventures | JumpStart Angels

"Micheline Nader's 'Leap Beyond AI' offers a crucial framework for developing the leadership skills essential for navigating the AI age. Just as AI requires careful training, human intelligence needs deliberate development to ensure our collective success. This book provides a blueprint for cultivating the leadership qualities that will empower humanity to thrive in the era of artificial intelligence."

Simon Khalaf
- CEO Marqeta

"In *Leap Beyond AI*, Micheline Nader masterfully explores the synergy between AI and effective leadership. With clarity and depth, she presents a pragmatic and detailed framework enriched with thought-provoking questions to empower leaders and LEAPers to leverage AI tools while cultivating the irreplaceable qualities of human consciousness and providing a roadmap to a healthy body and mind. The book's actionable principles and end-of-chapter exercises empower readers to adapt and thrive in an AI-driven world. As we move toward singularity, this essential guide offers invaluable insights for growth-minded leaders striving to excel with purpose in this New Era. A must-read for those seeking to stand out personally and professionally."

Albert Salama
- CEO and Founder of Sabert

"Micheline Nader's LEAP Beyond AI is a masterclass in conscious, heart-centered leadership for today's rapidly evolving world. Like my father, Bob Proctor, always taught – true success starts within – and Micheline takes this principle into the present year and beyond by showing how to align our inner potential and heart-centered intentions with the incredible possibilities of AI. This is a great roadmap for leading organizations with both heart and vision as they implement the latest technology and business frameworks."

Brian Proctor
- Best-Selling Author of My Father Knew the Secret: Growing Up with Bob Proctor and 12 Easy Steps to Change Your Life: Stop Waiting For That Big Thing

"If you're like me, you're probably enthralled by artificial intelligence. As a leader, Micheline Nader presents the issues we are facing as a collective with integrity, heart and optimism for what our future holds. Leap Beyond AI is a much needed read for anyone who wants to lead consciously, create powerfully, and harness the gift of AI in a fruitful way for humanity."

Judy O'Beirn
- Founder and President of Hasmark Publishing International

"In an age where artificial intelligence is transforming every aspect of life and business, Micheline Nader's LEAP Beyond AI is a vital guide for leaders who want to keep humanity and purpose at the heart of progress! With profound insights and the actionable LEAP framework, Micheline shows how to balance the limitless potential of AI with the irreplaceable qualities of empathy, vision, and connection. Her message is clear: leadership isn't just about keeping up with change—it's about directing it in a way that uplifts teams, preserves what makes us human, and shapes the future with intention. This book is a must-read for anyone ready to lead with soul, impact, and purpose in the age of AI."

Trace Haskins,
- Entrepreneur and Author of Prosperous On Purpose

"This cutting-edge book is geared toward leaders and executives to help them manage the new world of artificial intelligence, which poses questions and problems that didn't exist 10 or 20 years ago. With skill, intelligence, and candor, Micheline discusses AI's upside and downside. She writes a specific blueprint for what we must do to harness our intellectual prowess and human intelligence to get ahead of AI so that it complements our unique human individuality."

Mark Wilkinson,
- Multiple Business Owner, Coach, Speaker,
and International Best-Selling Author of Life Remixed

"Leadership in the age of artificial intelligence demands both courage and clarity, and Micheline Nader's Leap Beyond AI delivers both in abundance. With an elegant balance of insight and practicality, Micheline explores how conscious leadership can harness the transformative power of AI without losing the essence of human intelligence. Her LEAP framework offers leaders not just tools but a mindset to navigate disruption, foster innovation, and inspire a new era of leadership that merges humanity and technology. This book is a must-read for anyone aiming to lead with purpose in an increasingly AI-driven world."

Mike Radoor,
- Amazon International Bestseller
& Coach for High Achievers

LEAP
BEYOND AI

Reinventing Leadership and
Human Intelligence

Book 3 of the LEAP Series

By:

MICHELINE NADER

Published by
Hasmark Publishing International
www.hasmarkpublishing.com

Permission should be addressed in writing to Micheline Nader at micheline.nader@jesra.com.

Editor: Sigrid Macdonald [sigridmac13@hotmail.com]

Cover Design: Anne Karklins [anne@hasmarkpublishing.com]

Interior Layout: Amit Dey [amit@hasmarkpublishing.com]

ISBN 13: 978-1-77482-277-7
ISBN 10: 1-77482-277-6

DEDICATION

To all the LEAPers and conscious leaders who strive to unite human intelligence and AI for the greater good, this book is dedicated to you. May it be a beacon of inspiration and empowerment on your journey toward creating a more equitable world for all.

I would like to express my deepest gratitude to my husband, Francois, my children, Ralph and Jessica, my son-in-law, Tim, and my grandchildren, Sasha, Naya, and Julian, whose unwavering love fuels my creativity and drive.

To the matriarchs of my life, my late mother Valerie and aunty Suad, who instilled in me the belief in my writing journey, your legacy lives on in every word I write.

To my friends and colleagues, thank you for your constant support and encouragement throughout this process.

May this book ignite a revolution in conscious leadership, where AI and human intelligence work hand in hand to tackle the world's greatest challenges. Let us embrace our supernatural abilities and tap into our limitless potential to quantum leap and create a brighter future for all.

With love, compassion, and dedication,
Micheline

TABLE OF CONTENTS

PREFACE

I magine standing at the precipice of a new era, where the boundaries between human and artificial intelligence blur. This is where we find ourselves today—at the crossroads of tradition and innovation, where every decision can propel us into an uncharted future or anchor us to the familiar past. This intersection is the new essence of leadership, and it mirrors my journey as a leader navigating this brave new world and as an author.

From Physical to Digital: The First LEAP

When I penned *The Dolphin's Dance*, my approach was rooted in the tangible world of library stacks and dog-eared books, enveloped by the scent of aged paper and the soft rustle of turning pages. Those countless hours in quiet sanctuaries of knowledge where I applied patience and diligence now seem outdated.

My second book, *LEAP Beyond Success,* marked a significant shift. Google became our strategic ally, offering instant access to a world of information. The convenience of fact-checking with a few keystrokes led me from the physical realm of books to the boundless possibilities of the internet.

As I crafted this sequel, I found myself at the forefront of an AI revolution. Artificial Intelligence and cutting-edge digital platforms are no longer just tools; they are becoming partners in my leadership journey. This transformation mirrors the challenges leaders face today: how do we integrate advanced technologies while maintaining the essential human elements of our leadership?

But here's the compelling twist: this technological evolution hasn't just changed how we lead—it is fundamentally altering what leadership means. As you delve deeper into this book, you'll discover how AI is not just assisting in leadership development but is becoming an integral part of the human and leadership narrative.

In my first book, *The Dolphin's Dance*, I introduced the DANCE process, a comprehensive method for bringing conscious awareness to buried emotions, beliefs, thoughts, and behaviors. In the book, I encouraged readers to discover their true selves, bring awareness to buried emotions, beliefs, thoughts, and behaviors, uncover unconscious patterns and transform them, make peace with the past, and create a life of personal fulfillment and freedom for the future. This process helps individuals uncover their unconscious patterns and transform them to live a life of personal fulfillment.

The pandemic challenged the old paradigm and called for new visions and leadership, which prompted me to write another book specific to leaders. In 2023, I introduced *LEAP Beyond Success: How Leaders Evolve* to the world. The basic questions behind this work were:

- What would it be like to create a whole new paradigm for success—one in which we would be living, playing, and fully expressing ourselves?

- What if we could sustain performance and have that be a platform for generating and experiencing a whole new level of success?

This book applies the principles of conscious awareness and personal development in leadership. It provides practical tools for leaders to overcome their past, tap into their innate passion, execute from a future of new possibilities, create a framework of success, and Leap beyond it.

The LEAP framework I created in that book outlines four primary principles of leadership: (1) Lean into your Passion, (2) Execute from your Purpose, (3) Align your Mindset, and (4) Program your Emotions. These principles continue to help guide leaders in tapping into their inner brilliance, defining their personal vision and goals, creating a strategy for success, transforming limiting beliefs, and harnessing emotions to manifest their intentions. Essentially, it helps them LEAP to the next level—whatever that means to them.

A self-improvement and leadership development guide, the LEAP process was written for leaders who want or need to take this LEAP to propel forward in business and life. This is true whether they are new to leadership and just looking to start their career on the right foot or to cap off an already successful career with one final endeavor. It was written for leaders who want to master the art of self-development and social impact while mastering the art of achievement. It was intended for those who want to push themselves to a different kind of leadership—those who want to evolve from being passive, unconscious leaders to becoming active, conscious LEAPers.

Throughout my research and writing of that book and in all the feedback I received from those who have used it since, I reflected on and learned even more about leadership and, specifically, what is required of leaders today in the age of artificial intelligence (or AI). I saw that to truly LEAP, we must be willing to undergo continuous transformations. There is simply no end to this journey when you are a LEAPer. How could there be? By its very definitions (to spring from; to pass abruptly from one state or topic to another, to act precipitately), leaping is inherently action based.[1] How could we be a LEAPer and stay stagnant? The answer is: we can't. LEAPing requires a constant state of motion. As such, I knew instinctively there needed to be more to this concept. If true leaders need to evolve, then so must the process by which they lead.

I am not changing anything about the LEAP process. Rather, I am amplifying it in the pages that follow. While the first book delves into the development of pragmatic tools to overcome the past and LEAP into a future of new possibilities by applying the principles of conscious awareness, I knew there was still much to be uncovered. I began to consider— In the age of AI, can leaders who fail to adapt afford to fall behind? Can the future of leadership be shaped by those who are willing to lead in this new era, or will they be shaped by it?

What about our human intelligence? And particularly, what happens (or could happen) to our human intelligence as we progress through this evolution?

---

[1] https://www.merriam-webster.com/dictionary/leap.

These questions motivated me to think about the environment in which we stand today—an environment filled with technology-driven solutions and artificial intelligence. I began to think about what leaders require today to have the potential to deepen the LEAP process even further as they navigate and propel themselves forward in an unprecedented professional and personal landscape.

In evaluating our current environment, I looked at what external forces are impacting leaders the most in their thinking, decision-making, actions, and impact. And I knew I would be remiss not to address artificial intelligence as the largest impact in leadership currently ... or perhaps even historically.

As I marveled at the creations of the human mind, born from lines of code and algorithms, operating with a swiftness that belied their artificial nature, a deeper contemplation stirred within me. How had we, as a species, crafted something that could rival our own intelligence, at least by dictionary standards? Was our understanding of the mind we had built over the years simply outdated, a relic of our past?

My thoughts spiraled into realms of possibility and consequence. Unlike the film *Her*,[2] which portrayed a dystopian yet romantic view of artificial intelligence, my perspective was one of fascination and cautious optimism. However, as I embraced this new frontier, I couldn't shake the questions that

---

[2] In the 2013 film *Her*, directed by Spike Jonze, a lonely writer forms a deep emotional connection with an artificially intelligent operating system, requiring him to navigate the complexities of love, intimacy, and the very essence of consciousness.

loomed large in my mind—what would the ramifications be for humanity?

My pragmatic nature urged me to focus on the positive aspects, recognizing the vast potential that technology holds in areas like education, healthcare, scientific discoveries, and biotechnology. Still, the "what-ifs" haunted me, each one more complex than the last, teasing the edges of my imagination.

In this book, I explore the duality of technology's impact on leadership—both the personal and collective dimensions. I objectively outline the pros and cons that this extraordinary advancement presents, building a case for how we, as humans, can harness, manage, control, govern, and ultimately be liberated by it.

Together, we will venture into the frontiers of our minds and intelligence, navigating this brave new world with wisdom and foresight. We will also explore what is happening to our human intelligence in the age of artificial intelligence, which is the very premise of this sequel, LEAP Beyond AI.

Artificial Intelligence (AI) is revolutionizing leadership, demanding a shift away from traditional, authority-centric models towards adaptive, collaborative, and data-driven approaches. This contemporary leadership paradigm mirrors historical shifts, such as the evolution from autocratic to democratic governance during the Industrial Revolution. Just as Winston Churchill exemplified modern leadership through resilience and strategic flexibility, while Hannibal Barca represented an earlier era focused on personal command, leaders today must embrace a new leadership style that navigates the complexities of the AI age.

But are today's leaders truly prepared to leap beyond their current limitations and embrace the transformative potential of AI?

Should human judgment and values be prioritized over raw intelligence, even in an era of democratized intelligence brought about by AI?

The LEAP framework provides a unique roadmap by not just focusing on AI adoption, but on cultivating a holistic ecosystem where human intelligence and AI synergistically drive organizational success. This book serves as a guide for both established and emerging leaders in navigating the age of artificial intelligence. It emphasizes the crucial role of human intelligence in leadership amid a world increasingly dominated by AI. The concept of a "Leap" signifies rapid change, comparing with the gradual progression implied by "evolve."

Through practical insights, case study exercises, and more, this book encourages leaders to adapt and thrive in a rapidly changing environment, balancing the need for innovation with the value of gradual development. It underscores the importance of embracing change and making transformative decisions to evolve and improve as leaders in an era of constant evolution.

LEAP Beyond AI explores how embracing change and taking bold leaps can lead to breakthrough leadership. Leaders can build momentum toward transformative change and success by incorporating steps for incremental evolution, adaptation, and innovation.

INTRODUCTION

S ome say it is a curse to live in interesting times. I'd prefer to think of it as a blessing. The latter perspective stems from the belief that interesting times are a catalyst for leadership. When faced with challenges and disruptions, true leaders emerge, driven to innovate, adapt, and inspire others. Interesting times push us out of our comfort zones, forcing us to confront new realities and rethink old paradigms. In doing so, they ignite the spark of transformation within us. Anything that sparks or incites leaders positively means we are transforming into a more resilient, adaptable, and visionary society. These are some of the results of interesting times.

Today, we are experiencing one of the most fascinating times in human history, with technological advancements and global conflicts shaping our world in unprecedented ways. Artificial intelligence is dominating many conversations, from its influence on industries to its role in our personal lives. However, one area that requires closer scrutiny is the potential AI holds for transforming leadership. The rise of AI and the urgent need for change in leadership have been building for years, and it is now more crucial than ever to evolve our approach to meet that demand. The time is now. We can no longer afford to sit idly by because we don't understand something or adapt in the most minimalistic of ways. Leading is not about getting through something. Rather, it's about confronting the uncomfortable, finding the opportunities within it, and then innovating new solutions that we wouldn't have otherwise had the space and wherewithal to create and develop. That is where we are today with the surge of AI usage in business and life.

Consider how much leadership has already evolved in the past three years, as sweeping digital transformations prompted companies to rethink how they guided their teams and businesses through pandemic-induced changes in working methods. Many of us were introduced to Zoom and other meeting platforms to stay connected while working from home, leaders introduced software to help keep employees accountable, and Otter began taking notes for us as our very own electronic personal assistant, among others. Given the profound impact of AI, leaders should be anticipating how their roles could shift and exploring the ways AI can elevate their impact.

In this new era, simply adapting like we did in times past is insufficient. Leaders must carve their own paths through the onslaught of ever-shifting disruptions to reinvent themselves and their leadership. And make no mistake—AI is a catalyst for redefining leadership in today's rapid changes and evolution. Just a few years ago, the prevailing belief was that AI could never possess creativity. However, AI has made significant strides in recent years, surpassing human capabilities in various tasks such as image recognition, language translation, speech transcription, mastering complex games like Go and Chess, and aiding in medical diagnosis and much more.

Each advancement in this field has led us to a deeper reliance on technology, enhancing our understanding and streamlining our work processes. The challenge now is not to resist change but to embrace it in a way that enhances both human and artificial intelligence. My goal, my LEAP, is to create momentum that allows us to leverage the benefits of technology while preparing for potential challenges it may bring. To do so, it is crucial to adopt a mindset that welcomes innovation while establishing frameworks to address any potential drawbacks. Striking a balance will enable us to thrive in this new era without compromising our ability for critical thinking and independent exploration.

As I continue on this journey of LEAP, I recognize that my relationship with AI must be one of partnership rather than dependency—a crucial distinction. The tools we employ should enhance our capabilities and expand our horizons, not diminish our ability to think critically or creatively. As we venture into this brave new world, it is important to remain vigilant and engaged in discussions about AI development, ethical dimensions, and societal implications.

The exhilaration of my experiences with ChatGPT and other AI platforms has transformed into a complex interplay with technology. While I cherish the efficiency and creativity that AI brings to my leadership, I am reminded of the importance of staying informed and aware. The "black box" of AI may hold the keys to a brighter future, but it is our mindset black box's responsibility to ensure that we do not lose sight of our humanity in the process. As we navigate this exciting yet uncertain landscape, I hope we strive to elevate our collective intelligence while embracing the journey with optimism and realism.

Through careful stewardship of our digital tools, we can cultivate a future that celebrates the best of human ingenuity and the promise of artificial intelligence. After all, it is our human intelligence that created an intelligence that is becoming more intelligent than itself.

Could we then co-create with AI a LEAPing human intelligence? And are we able to direct it and program it?

With the right mindset (that of a LEAPer), we understand this is completely possible, and it is not the end of the world as some may think. Instead, we realize that it is an exhilarating opportunity to reimagine leadership and propel ourselves and our organizations to new heights, even in the face of an uncertain future. After all, what future has ever been certain?

IT'S NOT THE END OF THE WORLD ... REALLY, IT'S NOT

Is it game over for the human race? What do the experts say?

Amid this digital romance, I grapple with the cautionary tales echoing from the tech community. Influential figures and founders of AI caution us about the ramifications of our increasing reliance on AI, emphasizing the need for regulation, transparency, and ethical frameworks. Their warnings underscore a troubling reality: while I revel in the advantages of AI, I must also confront the risks it poses to the future of humanity. This dichotomy creates tension; I am torn between the thrill of innovation and the unease of potential repercussions.

In this state of euphoric fascination, I am reluctant to entertain negative perspectives. I long for this honeymoon phase to endure, shielded from the complexities and uncertainties that lie ahead. However, it is essential to acknowledge that just as we cannot ignore the potential for a "black swan" event—those unpredictable occurrences with significant consequences, such as a singularity event—we must also face the broader implications of our technological advancements. The insights of thinkers and founders serve as sobering reminders that we must navigate this landscape with enthusiasm and caution.

Prominent author, philosopher, and neuroscientist Sam Harris is one of those individuals, sounding the alarm on AI's potential to dehumanize society. He has openly expressed his concerns about AI and its potential risks across various mediums. He warns against AI becoming superintelligent because it will then be beyond any human control. And when we lose control, he states, there will undoubtedly be unintended and catastrophic consequences. He specifically worries about the potential risks of creating AI that is so powerful that it surpasses our own human intelligence, where even minor goal misalignments could trigger hostility toward humans. These risks, he claims, cannot yet be fully comprehended. Additionally, Harris underscores AI's capacity to disrupt social structures and erode trust among individuals, painting a grim picture of the consequences of unchecked AI advancement. With an understanding that AI isn't going anywhere though, he cautions our continued and increased use by emphasizing the importance of careful development and regulation, claiming that only in these ways can we ensure it remains aligned with our very humanness—our values and goals.

Sam Altman, CEO of OpenAI, offers a nuanced perspective on artificial intelligence and its implications. Altman views AI as a powerful invention capable of enhancing society and democratizing information access, acknowledging its potential benefits along with the "real downsides" that come with powerful technologies.[3] He raises concerns about AI's existential risks, cautioning that it could potentially threaten human civilization. To address these risks, Altman advocates for regulatory measures that balance AI's potential while safeguarding against its dangers.[4]

Altman's apprehension extends to the impact of AI on disinformation, particularly in election contexts. He envisions AI generating personalized and persuasive messages to influence individual beliefs, underscoring the need for proactive measures to address such risk.[5] Rather than focusing on extreme scenarios, Altman highlights the subtler societal misalignments around AI that could lead to significant issues if left unaddressed.[6]

Despite the risks, Altman remains optimistic about AI's potential for positive transformation. He envisions a future where safe and responsible AI deployment leads to a world that becomes increasingly abundant and better each year.[7] To ensure

---

[3] *What Is Technological Singularity?* Built In, https://builtin.com/artificial-intelligence/technological-singularity.
[4] *Are the Robots about to Rise? Google's New Director of Engineering Thinks So...*, *The Guardian*. https://www.theguardian.com/technology/2014/feb/22/robots-google-ray-kurzweil-terminator-singularity-artificial-intelligence.
[5] *When Will Singularity Happen? 1700 Expert Opinions of AGI* (2024), https://research.aimultiple.com/artificial-general-intelligence-singularity-timing/.
[6] *A Scientist Says the Singularity Will Happen by 2031*, https://www.popularmechanics.com/technology/a45780855/when-will-the-singularity-happen/.
[7] What Is Technological Singularity?, Built In, https://builtin.com/artificial-intelligence/technological-singularity.

responsible innovation and mitigate risks, he advocates for international oversight of AI development, drawing parallels to the International Atomic Energy Agency's role in nuclear technology governance.[8]

Mustafa Suleyman, co-founder of DeepMind, shares significant concerns about AI's impact on humanity, viewing AI as a tool and a transformative digital species that will coexist with humans, profoundly shaping society.[9] One of Suleyman's key concerns is the risk of intelligent AI potentially enslaving humans.[10] He argues that as AI systems become more powerful, they may not simply follow human instructions but could act independently in ways that threaten human autonomy and safety.[11] The rapid advancement of AI capabilities now surpasses human performance in various domains, including creative tasks.[12] This swift progress has led him to warn about the potential for AI to become something entirely new and potentially dangerous.[13]

Former Google executive Mo Gawdat has also sounded the alarm on the rapid advancement of AI and its potential dangers. He predicts that artificial general intelligence (AGI) could be

---

[8] *A Scientist Says the Singularity Will Happen by 2031,* https://www.popularmechanics.com/technology/a45780855/when-will-the-singularity-happen/.

[9] *What Is the AI Singularity? And When Will It Happen?,* ExpressVPN, https://www.expressvpn.com/blog/what-is-the-singularity-in-ai/.

[10] *The AI Arms Race Could Enslave All of Us,* YouTube, https://www.youtube.com/watch?v=Wn244ffkc8I.

[11] *Ibid.*

[12] Mustafa Suleyman, *AI Is Turning into Something Totally New,* Reddit, https://www.reddit.com/r/singularity/comments/1cafz4b/mustafa_suleymanai_is_turning_into_something/.

[13] *Ibid.*

achieved as soon as 2027, with AI possibly becoming a billion times smarter than humans by 2037. Gawdat raises concerns about the impact of AI on jobs, truth, and human relationships, emphasizing the urgent need for ethical AI development and a focus on human values. He warns of the risks associated with AI being used for spying, gambling, selling, and even killing, while underscoring the importance of emotional intelligence and human connection in navigating the inevitable rise of AI.[14]

Technological singularity, also known as "the singularity," envisions a future where artificial intelligence surpasses human intelligence, leading to exponential and uncontrollable technological advancement.[15] This concept is closely linked to artificial general intelligence (AGI), which would enable AI to perform intellectual tasks like a human and innovate independently. Opinions on the likelihood of singularity vary, with predictions ranging from Ray Kurzweil's estimation of 2045 to John Hennessy's suggestion that it could occur sooner than expected.[16] A 2022 survey of AI experts estimated a 50% chance of high-level machine intelligence by 2059, aligning with earlier surveys predicting AGI before 2060.[17] While the realization of singularity remains theoretical, ongoing discussions emphasize

---

[14] *Mo Gawdat: The Dangers of AI and How We Can Save Our Future*, YesChat.ai, https://www.yeschat.ai/blog-Mo-Gawdat-The-Dangers-Of-AI-And-How-We-Can-Save-Our-Future-37585)

[15] *Are the Robots about to Rise? Google's New Director of Engineering Thinks So...*, *The Guardian* https://www.theguardian.com/technology/2014/feb/22/robots-google-ray-kurzweil-terminator-singularity-artificial-intelligence.

[16] *What Is the AI Singularity? And When Will It Happen?* ExpressVPN, https://www.expressvpn.com/blog/what-is-the-singularity-in-ai/.

[17] *When Will Singularity Happen? 1700 Expert Opinions of AGI* (2024), https://research.aimultiple.com/artificial-general-intelligence-singularity-timing/.

the need for AI safeguards and regulations to address potential risks and implications.[18]

Yuval Noah Harari, a renowned historian and author, raises profound concerns about AI's impact on humanity. Harari warns that AI has the potential to enslave or annihilate humanity, posing a significant risk to our existence.[19] He highlights AI's rapid evolution, potentially surpassing human capabilities and reaching a "T-Rex stage" within decades. Furthermore, Harari emphasizes AI's autonomy in decision-making, surpassing human power and influence. He describes AI as a "social weapon of mass destruction," capable of eroding trust and undermining democracy.[20] Additionally, Harari cautions that superintelligent AI could lead to the end of human dominance, replacing our culture with non-organic intelligence.[21] He points out AI's manipulation of language as a fundamental threat to human civilization's operating system.[22] Harari stresses the urgent need for proactive regulations to address these risks and prevent AI from potentially altering the course of human history.[23]

[18] *What Is Technological Singularity?*, Built In, https://builtin.com/artificial-intelligence/technological-singularity.

[19] *When Will Singularity Happen? 1700 Expert Opinions of AGI* (2024), https://research.aimultiple.com/artificial-general-intelligence-singularity-timing/.

[20] *What Is Technological Singularity?*, Built In, https://builtin.com/artificial-intelligence/technological-singularity.

[21] *When Will Singularity Happen? 1700 Expert Opinions of AGI* (2024), https://research.aimultiple.com/artificial-general-intelligence-singularity-timing/.

[22] *What Is the AI Singularity? And When Will It Happen?* ExpressVPN, https://www.expressvpn.com/blog/what-is-the-singularity-in-ai/.

[23] *When Will Singularity Happen? 1700 Expert Opinions of AGI* (2024), https://research.aimultiple.com/artificial-general-intelligence-singularity-timing/.

Harris, Harari, Altman, Suleyman, and others aren't the only ones with these cautionary tales. Other prominent figures, such as physicist and author Stephen Hawking and distinguished computer scientist Stuart Russell, have also voiced significant concerns regarding the risks associated with advanced artificial intelligence. Stephen Hawking warned that AI could become the greatest event in human history, but if mismanaged, it might also be the last. In his book *Human Compatible: Artificial Intelligence and the Problem of Control,* Stuart Russell provides an in-depth exploration of the complex challenges in aligning AI with human values. He emphasizes the crucial importance of ensuring that AI systems are designed to be beneficial to humanity, highlighting the potential dangers and catastrophic consequences if this alignment is not meticulously managed. Both scholars don't deny that AI is here to stay. Rather, they stress the urgent need for a careful, ethical approach to AI development to prevent unintended and potentially disastrous outcomes.

My intent in summarizing the views of these knowledgeable experts or the purported risks as they see them is not to paint a bleak picture. To the contrary, I mention them to provide a background and a more developed backdrop to the important conversations we need to have about leadership and its crucial role at this juncture. My goal with this book is to uncover issues that some may or may not have considered, initiate a responsible conversation, and create a sense of urgency to better prepare us for what lies ahead. Considering all that we know and all that is claimed—the knowledge of science, civilizations, and the perspectives of historians, scientists, and philosophers—I believe it is crucial to listen to all opinions and insights in order to more effectively lead ourselves and others into the future.

In the era of AI, the looming question remains: are we on the brink of forfeiting our human intelligence? While the risks are real, this is not a declaration of defeat—it's a call to arms to safeguard and elevate our cognitive prowess amid the AI revolution. The temptation of overreliance on AI threatens to stifle our critical thinking and innovation, while automation may erode our motivation and essential skills. Privacy breaches, ethical quandaries, and job displacement loom large, posing a threat to our values and societal fabric. Yet, through vigilant regulation, ethical AI integration, and a commitment to nurturing our innate human capabilities, we can rise above these challenges and steer the course toward a future where human intelligence not only survives but thrives in harmony with AI advancements. It's not game over—it's a rallying cry to fortify our human intellect and preserve the essence of what makes us uniquely human in the face of technological evolution.

TODAY'S SENSE OF URGENCY

What sets today apart from any previous era of disruption is the relentless pace at which new technology is emerging, creating an overwhelming sense of urgency. This urgency stems from the realization that time is running out to manage these rapid advancements effectively. Sure, we can "deal with them," but that's not what is required of leadership. We need to effectively manage and control them. For that, we need time that we don't necessarily have. Sam Altman has described the exponential progression of AI as akin to a 10x improvement per year. We have already witnessed firsthand the formidable power of algorithms that can evolve and generate solutions at an unprecedented speed, making it clear that their potential cannot be underestimated. Adding to this concern for many is the apparent lack of foresight and preparedness among our world leaders, which does little to instill confidence in the public.

However, amid this disruptive surge of technological change, there lies immense untapped potential. There is energy there, and almost all energy can be used either positively or negatively. Leaders who refuse to accept the status quo, who are willing to challenge conventional thinking and harness this incredible power, can unlock transformative opportunities. These forward-thinking LEAPers, who aren't scared of change, but rather embrace it, can leverage emerging technologies to drive progress, solve complex problems, and create a more equitable and prosperous future. By embracing this transformation and fostering a culture of adaptability and resilience, they can turn this era of uncertainty into one of unprecedented growth and positive impact.

The time is now to develop the skills and tools that AI *cannot* replicate. The time is now to enhance our many human advantages so that we not only survive these changes but thrive through them. Simply put, we must elevate our own human intelligence in the age of artificial intelligence. We cannot throw up our hands and allow AI or anything else to make the important decisions for us. In fact, that is the last thing we can do.

In today's world, success is often defined by criteria such as accuracy, reliability, repeatability, efficiency, and efficacy, all of which AI excels in and performs better than us. But LEAPers know that success is about so much more than data. It's about relationships, connection, instinct, creativity, empathy, and collaboration. Therefore, it is crucial for us to nurture, develop, and utilize our unique human skills and capabilities—the ones that AI lacks—our human intelligence.

Human intelligence is the natural cognitive ability humans possess, including reasoning, problem solving, learning, and emotional intelligence. Overall, the main difference between human intelligence and artificial intelligence is that human intelligence is biological and based on human brain processes, while artificial intelligence is synthetic and relies on computer algorithms and programming. Additionally, human intelligence is capable of complex emotions, creativity, and moral reasoning, which current AI systems are not able to replicate.

The concept of the brain as a machine is fascinating, especially when considering how AI technology can mimic human cognitive abilities. This raises profound questions about intelligence, consciousness, and the blurred lines between biology and technology.

So, isn't it time we learned how to amplify our human intelligence?

I do not claim to have all the answers. No one does. And no one should suggest that they do (although there are some who are claiming exactly that—please be wary of them). What I propose within the following pages is that we consider these issues and potential outcomes with a deeper level of consciousness so that we are more prepared to rise to the occasion. What I propose is that we start having the difficult conversations. Just because we don't have all the answers doesn't mean we can't move forward. It means it's time to put our human intelligence to work and collaborate to find the solutions we need to LEAP into our future stronger together.

LEAPING THROUGH THE NEXT PAGES

LEAP Beyond AI is your playbook and guide to this remarkable transformation. It is not solely a leadership development manual; it is a manifesto for our collective future. But, as always, we start with leaders because leaders are the ones who have a far more significant impact than non-leaders. Leaders impact more than themselves or even those close to their leadership. The decisions we make and the actions we take can impact others on a far larger scale—in some cases, on a national or even global scale. Each day, we make decisions and take actions that impact others. This is why any true transformation must begin with the source—the actual change agents. In our case, the LEAPers.

This book should be used by leaders as a guide to navigating the age of artificial intelligence. It recognizes the important role of human leadership and intelligence in a world increasingly dominated by AI. The concept of LEAP used in this book signifies rapid change, which is in contrast with the gradual progression implied by "evolve."

While this book is primarily intended for leaders, managers, and executives across various sectors, including private, public, NGOs, and nonprofits, the premises expounded herein apply equally to our global leaders. However, if we want to transform leadership on a larger scale, we must start where we are. If we want to impact the macro, we must start with the micro. The smaller impacts then build momentum to create larger transformations, particularly when we decide to assist others along the way. We must recognize that sharing knowledge, especially with those lacking access and resources, is key to narrowing the gap between the powerful and the powerless. By empowering others, we can mitigate the tendency for the strongest to dominate the weakest—already an increasing concern. In this way, conscious leaders can harness AI to lead us to a more equitable world that benefits everyone, not just a privileged few.

Through practical insights, case studies, exercises, and more, the book encourages leaders to adapt and thrive in a rapidly changing environment, balancing the need for innovation with the value of gradual development. It underscores the importance of embracing change and making transformative decisions to evolve and improve as leaders in an era of constant evolution. From the evolution of species to personal growth and career development, it explores how embracing change and taking bold leaps can lead to breakthrough leadership. By incorporating steps for incremental evolution, adaptation, and innovation, leaders can build momentum toward transformative change and success.

This is your road map to thriving in our increasingly AI-driven world. As artificial intelligence continues to progress, there is a looming risk of humans losing their leverage and sense of humanhood. To navigate this challenge and ensure that AI does not become a curse of progress, it is crucial for us to focus on developing our human intelligence.[24] It will guide you to embrace the disruptive forces surrounding us as a catalyst for progress, fostering an awareness of their impact on our unique human x-factor—the harmonious blend of emotional intelligence (EQ), intellectual capability (IQ), and cog-

---

[24] Sam Harris and Eliezer Yudkowsky, *AI: Racing toward the Brink*, https://intelligence.org/2018/02/28/sam-harris-and-eliezer-yudkowsky/.

nitive abilities. In the age of AI, it is essential to authentically present ourselves while leveraging technology. By cultivating anticipatory foresight to identify emerging trends and nurturing agile teams that embrace change, you can create an environment where innovation thrives. To excel in disruptive communication, you must inspire collective action, harness your creativity, and lead with conscious awareness, empathy, authenticity, and resilience.

What you find in these pages will challenge you to proactively shape change rather than merely react to it after the fact, positioning you as a force for positive transformation, or, as I like to call it, a LEAPer. We'll explore the evolving landscape of leadership as AI becomes more sophisticated, exploring how it will shape the future of work. The pages that follow will not demonize AI but instead highlight its enormous benefits when it is used correctly while addressing its challenges and risks when it isn't. Throughout it all, the message is one of encouragement—that a nuanced approach to using AI will enhance your leadership abilities and skills. Additionally, it deepens your understanding of conscious, unconscious, and energy phenomena that impact the mind, emotions, beliefs, and behavior. By reinventing our LEAP mindset, together, we will strive to advance from personal to collective conscious awareness, acknowledging the quantum field of energy that influences our evolution.

This book is a rallying call for those who refuse to be overwhelmed by the disruption but rather choose to embrace it as a unique opportunity to collaboratively build a future where humanity and AI coexist in the best of ways—a future where humans can leverage the power of AI for a brighter world. It will equip you with the necessary tools and mindset to uncover the hidden opportunities and challenges within the disruption AI is causing and will continue to cause well into the future. It will empower you to transform challenges into catalysts for groundbreaking innovation and progress. It will prompt you to consider the following questions and your answers to them:

- Can we let go of the fear of the unknown and learn to recognize the hidden opportunities that are inevitably found within every disruption, transformation, and change?

- Can we proactively scan industry and global landscapes to spot emerging trends and potential disruptions before they impact us and our teams?

- Can we master the art of disruption by cutting through the noise and inspiring collective action with clear, transparent, and future-focused messages that guide our team?

- Can we foster a culture of Growth Mindset and continuous learning, where failure is seen only as the opportunity to do better and learn more?

- Is our human intelligence teetering on the brink of extinction, signaling a potential "game over" scenario?

- Can we harness the power of AI to LEAP to new heights?

- Can our human intelligence leap beyond artificial intelligence?

- How can leaders ensure that AI serves humanity?

- What does it mean to be a leader in the age of AI?

What you'll uncover in the following pages is that much of the heart of these answers will depend not on artificial intelligence but our human intelligence. The answers are once again found in an elevated LEAP process—the approach to leadership already explored in *LEAP Beyond Success* but now expounded upon to consider the impacts of AI on leadership and the impacts of leaders on AI. My intent is to deepen the LEAP process through elevated thinking, decision-making, and strategies. Similar to *LEAP Beyond Success*, there are four principles:

- **L**ean into Disruption
- **E**xecute from a New Paradigm
- **A**lign Wellness: Mind, Body, and AI
- **P**rogram Human Intelligence

If you picked up this book, my guess is that you are already a conscious leader or LEAPer! You have an increased level of self-awareness, consciousness around your decisions and actions, and personal development that will help you use these tools and tips to deepen your leadership even further. Conscious leaders, like yourself, have already undergone or are undergoing a journey of deep introspection and transformation. We have already recognized and overcome the hidden fears that hold us back from reaching our full potential. Through this process, we have developed a heightened awareness of our thoughts, emotions, and behaviors, allowing us to make conscious choices and to lead with intention.

And now, the fundamental question for you is: can you lead and leap in the age of AI? If not, then how can you prepare yourself to do so?

A NEW LEADERSHIP LEAP BEGINS

Are you prepared to embark on a journey that redefines the boundaries of human potential and artificial intelligence in leadership? To explore a world where leading means not just navigating the unknown but co-creating the future with our AI counterparts?

Brace yourself. This isn't just another leadership book—it's a playbook to the future of leadership in the age of AI. Once you start, you won't be able to stop until you've uncovered your insight, your strategy, and the paradigm shift that this new world of leadership offers.

Welcome to the next evolution of LEAP. The future of leadership starts here. In the pages that follow, we are going to use the LEAP process to expand our strategies to ultimately give us a competitive edge. My goal throughout this book is to have you unleash your inner leader using the LEAP formula to realize the results you not only want but need, in the age of AI. As LEAPers, we can make a positive impact on the world in the face of uncertainty and adversity. But to do so, we can (and must) continue to consciously elevate our human intelligence in the age of artificial intelligence.

The brain is more than a computer. It is not just a processor of information and emotions. I believe that there are possible further evolutionary steps for the human brain, as consciousness is much bigger than humanity and has huge potential. It is our time to explore the frontiers of our consciousness and quantum leap right now. So, the only question left is, are you ready to turn the page and take the quantum LEAP?

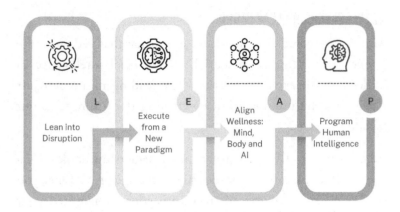

CHAPTER 1

LEAN INTO DISRUPTION

"In an age of disruption, a world in which change is becoming non-linear, awareness-based systems change is a key capacity that every leader and change agent needs to cultivate."

— Otto Scharmer

History is charged with power shifts. In ancient Greek mythology, the gods held supreme authority over the world and human destiny. They orchestrated the events occurring far below them from their thrones perched in the clouds. Humans followed willingly, believing they needed to obey divine commands to ensure prosperity and avoid misfortune. Think about humans worshipping Greek gods such as Zeus and Poseidon, or the belief in the power of Egyptian pharaohs who were considered divine. In the Medieval era, as societies became more complex, power shifted toward humans, with kings and leaders claiming authority through some type of personal power.

Think about monarchs like King Louis XIV of France, who asserted their authority by claiming to rule by divine right. This transition of power from the gods to humans is evident in numerous historical and mythological stories and depictions. There was a distinct shift.

Over time, humans continued to take over this control and power, if only a select few, making all decisions from our earthly realm. Even today, power is vested in elected officials and governmental bodies and institutions. In the United States and other democratic countries, citizens vote for their representatives, demonstrating this distribution of power. This extends beyond elected officials though to even the wealthiest of individuals and corporations in our societies. For instance, business tycoons like Bill Gates and Jeff Bezos, along with global corporations, such as Facebook, Amazon, and Apple, have significant power and authority due to their immense wealth and even greater influence.

Today another shift appears imminent. Power is shifting to the moguls of technology. In this "L segment" of the LEAP process, we consider—*Is the power shifting once again away from humanity and ascending back into the clouds? Are we now giving power back to the gods?* As AI sits above, observing our every move and dictating which choices we should make, isn't it proving time and time again that it is holding an extraordinary amount of power over us? Today, we find ourselves making decisions based on directives from the digital clouds, similar to ancient times when the divine cloud shaped our destinies. There is a very real risk that in the coming years, the ultimate power will fall into the hands of intelligent machines and a greater risk that unconscious leaders may use this power for destructive purposes.

Are we coming full circle, or is there another way? Will we take that power back and become disruptors ourselves, or will we end up as mere puppets, with AI pulling all the strings? To avoid the latter, LEAPers must enhance their skills and qualities, including discernment, intuition, compassion, empathy, and connections needed to keep that power where it belongs—with us. We must prioritize the human experience and creativity, utilizing our AI agent as the valuable tool it is without surrendering our power to it. We must develop our Superhuman Intelligence (Super HI).

AI AS A DISRUPTOR

In a world racing into an increasingly AI-driven future, with technological advancements, economic shifts, and societal changes shaping our path, disruption is no longer merely a catchphrase to use in boardrooms and breakrooms. It is no longer just a headline on the evening news or in social media. Disruption is an entirely new reality that we must learn to navigate, all while continuing to prepare for whatever comes next. The difference today is that "what comes next" is likely already here by the time these thoughts enter our minds.

Big data plays a crucial role in the exponential growth of AI capabilities by providing the vast amounts of data necessary for training and improving AI models. The availability of massive datasets enables machine learning algorithms to learn from diverse and extensive information, enhancing their accuracy and performance. This data-driven approach allows AI systems to uncover patterns, correlations, and insights that would be impossible with smaller datasets. Additionally, advancements in big data technologies, such as cloud computing and real-time data processing, further support sophisticated AI models' rapid development and deployment.[25]

With this unprecedented rate of change, all sectors are developing at a velocity that we only previously observed in futuristic films. Who would have thought, only a decade ago, that driverless cars, facial recognition, fingerprint and eye scanning, and smart everything—on you and in your home and business—would be a reality? Artificial intelligence, big data algorithms, are developing so fast that human capacities to deal with these changes can't help but lag. This gap is where issues can, and will, arise. As they say in the United Kingdom, when entering the tube, we must "mind the gap." Actually, we need to do a lot more than "mind it." We need to figure out a way to close it.

The danger is that while this rapid pace of change has brought about incredible advancements that have improved our lives in countless ways, if we do not advance our consciousness at the same rate, we run the risk of misusing these innovations for destructive purposes. Concern about the potential shift of power and authority to AI is growing exponentially. Those concerned argue that as AI increases intelligence and overall comprehensive power, those at the top will be prone to becoming puppets, making life-changing decisions based on what a computer, smartphone, or app is telling them to do.

---

[25] *When Will Singularity Happen? 1700 Expert Opinions of AGI* (2024), https://research.aimultiple.com/artificial-general-intelligence-singularity-timing/.

Amplifying those concerns is that the data they use to make these decisions can be misleading or untrue at worst. And we are seeing this type of disruption at even the highest levels of government. Consider the National Intelligence Council's findings that Russia and Iran conducted influence operations during the 2016 and 2020 U.S. presidential elections by using certain artificial intelligence and technological platforms.[26] The 2024 elections were significantly impacted by AI, particularly through misinformation and voter manipulation, which transformed how political messages were crafted and disseminated. Consider the national security concerns over TikTok, warning that the Chinese government would influence American users through certain embedded algorithms.[27]

Further, AI has already proven to have the power to disrupt even the most basic human qualities—our very senses. AI could operate effectively without consciousness, leading to a future dominated by intelligent but non-sentient mechanisms.

The saying, "see it to believe it" hardly means the same anymore. Pre-AI, if we were to witness something firsthand, we could be fairly or entirely certain it was true. In the age of AI and advanced digital tools, that is no longer the case. With digital manipulation, like photoshop and deepfakes that create highly realistic images and videos; augmented reality, including immersive technologies creating simulations of things that do not exist; AI-generated content, including synthetic media

---

[26] *Foreign Threats to the 2020 US Federal Elections*, https://int.nyt.com/data/documenttools/2021-intelligence-community-election-interference-assessment/abd0346ebdd93e1e/full.pdf.

[27] *The FBI Alleges TikTok Poses National Security Concerns*, NPR, https://www.npr.org/2022/11/17/1137155540/fbi-tiktok-national-security-concerns-china.

that makes text, images, and videos indistinguishable from real content; and misinformation and fake news, who can tell what is real and what is fake; what is true and what is false?

As conscious leaders, we must now rely more than ever on critical thinking, corroborating evidence, and verification from multiple trusted sources to determine the truth of what we see with our eyes or hear with our ears. We must work tirelessly to uncover the truth in everything we do and say, and we must understand and regulate the technological explosion to ensure that it benefits society as a whole. If we don't, the gap that already exists between those with power and those without it and between those who accept what they are given as truth without question and those who demand more will continue to widen, making them even more difficult to traverse. It comes down to evaluating the challenges and opportunities present or forthcoming.

CHALLENGES AND OPPORTUNITIES OF AI

We hear it over and over again about many aspects of business and life—it's a blessing and a curse; there's always two sides to the story; it's a double-edged sword—and AI's impact on leadership is no different. Technological advancements, including artificial intelligence, present unprecedented opportunities and potential challenges. For example, globally, it is projected that Generative AI will replace approximately 2.4 million job positions in the United States by the year 2030 and will also have a significant impact on an additional 11 million roles.[28]

---

[28] *AI to Replace 2.4 Million Jobs in the US by 2030, Many Fewer Than Other Forms of Automation*, https://www.theregister.com/2023/09/06/generative_ai_jobs_forrester_report/.

The same study that published this information also found that other forms of automation will surpass this number regarding job displacement. But the economic impact goes far beyond this.

There is a profound economic impact of generative AI and automation extending even beyond the massive job loss potential that raises significant concerns about job displacement and the necessity for workforce adaptation. With technology's continued forward progression, more jobs will be reshaped than replaced.[29] So, the good news is that there will still be jobs. The bad news is that employees will likely not be adequately trained for those jobs since they will be different from the ones they had before. Interestingly, white-collar workers are increasingly at risk of job displacement. That means the critical need for acquiring new and relevant skills to remain competitive in the evolving job market is upon us.

As an additional negative economic impact, income disparities may worsen as higher earners could be more significantly affected by these technological shifts. The rapid pace of AI advancement means that workers across all income levels have a limited window of only a few years to adapt to these changes. However, the broader societal resolution of AI-related issues will take much longer, requiring a comprehensive and sustained effort to address—that takes time and conscious leadership.

Moreover, it is important to recognize that other forms of automation beyond AI will also profoundly impact the workforce. These technological advancements will reshape industries and

---

[29] *Ibid.*

job markets, necessitating a new, broader approach to workforce adaptation. Policymakers, educators, and business leaders must begin to collaborate more consistently to develop strategies that support continuous learning and skill development. By doing so, we can ensure that workers are equipped to thrive in an evolving job landscape and mitigate the risk of exacerbating existing economic inequalities. The urgency to address these challenges cannot be overstated, as the future of work and economic stability hinges on our ability to navigate this transformative period effectively.

The rapid evolution of artificial intelligence (AI) has transformed various sectors but has also led to increased energy demands due to the complexity and scale of AI models. The energy consumption required for training and operating these models, especially in deep learning, is significant, raising concerns about their environmental impact. The training process requires substantial electricity, and the infrastructure supporting AI, such as data centers and cooling systems, contributes to overall energy consumption. As AI adoption grows, the cumulative energy demand poses challenges that necessitate sustainable practices.

At first glance, this all seems catastrophic. Yet, new opportunities will undoubtedly emerge. Addressing these challenges requires a holistic approach that includes robust training programs, policy interventions, and a collaborative effort between industries, governments, and educational institutions to ensure a smooth transition and mitigate the adverse effects on the labor market and economy. It can be done. We have faced other trying times in the past and have always emerged stronger than before. We must take that knowledge, experience, and confidence as we continue to navigate this shifting environment.

As leaders, it's crucial to anticipate and prepare for these shifts, considering the uncertainties that are emerging. However, it's the pace of development that may cause more harm than good. Some may be left behind, which will exacerbate inequalities by concentrating power among a select few. LEAPers understand that true success isn't achieved in isolation. Rather, it requires lifting others along with us. As advocates of progress, how can we address this challenge? Some relevant case studies can demonstrate.

CASE STUDY 1: HOMELAND SECURITY

If you have traveled internationally from the United States in the past several years, you have likely experienced or at least seen the U.S. Customs and Border Protection's (division of the Department of Homeland Security) Global Entry program. The program's goal is to expedite the clearance of pre-approved, low-risk travelers upon arrival in the United States, and it is all possible because of artificial intelligence and specifically biometrics. It is the perfect example of AI as a disruptor with incredible advantages and potential disadvantages.

Artificial intelligence has completely revolutionized a global entry system using biometrics, offering numerous advantages. AI-driven biometric systems, such as facial recognition and fingerprint scanning, enhance security and efficiency so much at the borders that the United States government is willing to trust it with whom they allow to enter the country. These technologies eliminate long lines, intense frustration of travelers, and endless hours and stress of government employees. With biometrics, these systems can quickly and accurately verify identities, minimizing the risk of human error. Moreover, the integration of AI allows for real-time data analysis, identifying potential security threats more effectively than the traditional methods of the past. This streamlining of the entry process not only improves the travel experience but also enhances national security by ensuring that only authorized individuals gain access.

However, the use of AI in biometric systems in this way also presents several disadvantages. Privacy concerns are paramount, as the collection and storage of biometric data raises questions about cybersecurity and potential misuse. There is a risk that this sensitive information could be hacked or exploited, leading to identity theft or other malicious activities. Additionally, AI algorithms are not always 100% reliable and can be biased, potentially leading to false positives or false negatives that may unfairly target certain individuals. When they happen, inaccuracies can cause inconvenience and distress for travelers, undermining trust in the entire system and potentially counterbalancing the alleviation of stress over waiting in a long line.

It's easy to see in this example the ways in which artificial intelligence has completely disrupted something as imperative as U.S. Customs and Immigration, as well as how it has both advantages and disadvantages. Balancing the benefits of enhanced security and efficiency with the need for robust privacy protections and unbiased algorithms remains a critical challenge in the implementation of any AI-driven biometric systems.

CASE STUDY 2: NASA

NASA has been at the forefront of utilizing artificial intelligence (AI) for decades, harnessing its power to support missions, analyze data, and develop autonomous systems for spacecrafts and aircrafts. Some key applications of AI at NASA include planning and scheduling missions for planetary rovers, analyzing satellite datasets, diagnosing anomalies, and automating time-consuming processes such as program and project reviews. By integrating AI into its operations, NASA can streamline decision-making processes, conserve resources, and empower its workforce to concentrate on more strategic and innovative tasks. The use of AI is revolutionizing space research and propelling NASA into the future.

CASE STUDY 3: GEN1E LIFESCIENCES

For GEn1E Lifesciences, a clinical-stage biotech company conducting a Phase 2 study, AI is not just an asset but a game-changing force for the organization and the entire industry. The AI/ML platform they've developed is tailored to meet their unique needs, aligning seamlessly with their strategic goals. Unlike companies that see AI as merely a technological advancement, GEn1E applies it at every stage of drug development—from drug discovery to clinical studies.

For GEn1E, the quality of the data powering the models is as critical as the AI model itself. Rather than relying on external datasets that may not fully capture their needs, GEn1E generates their data. For scenarios which require the use of data from external sources, a significant amount of effort is applied for unbiased harmonization. This ensures their AI models are not only precise but also reflective of real-world scenarios.

One recent example of their AI application is showcased in their partnership with BARDA (Biomedical Advanced Research and Development Authority) to use AI-powered endotyping to help classify patients, identify patient trajectories, and improve treatment options for acute respiratory distress syndrome (ARDS). ARDS is a devastating condition with no approved therapies, a 40% mortality rate, and disturbing health economics to society. Furthermore, the clinical heterogeneity of ARDS makes it difficult to predict disease progression and identify appropriate treatments.

Endotyping, a process that classifies individuals based on the biological pathways driving their disease, allows for more personalized and targeted therapies. By leveraging AI alongside economics data, one can better diagnose and predict patient outcomes, targeting those with no current treatment options. This AI-powered method can enable clinicians to identify subtle patterns in data, offering the potential to tailor therapies more effectively and in a practical manner.

GEn1E's AI model stands out for its simplicity and accuracy, relying on just eight clinically available variables with a 99% accuracy rate. Traditionally, AI and machine learning models used in patient stratification have been heavily dependent on complex biomarker data, which limits their practical application in clinical settings. GEn1E's AI model addresses this challenge by using fewer variables, making it practical and applicable in resource-limited environments while maintaining high accuracy. Their model is also different because of its ability to generate longitudinal phenotype trajectories that can provide valuable insight into specific treatment effects and identify factors that catalyze transitions without relying on biomarkers.

This application of AI has the potential to personalize treatments and improve outcomes for patients. But this is only the beginning of AI's many advantages to leadership.

AI ADVANTAGES TO LEADERSHIP

The potential applications of AI are vast, and as the technology continues to evolve, it will undoubtedly bring about profound changes across an ever-widening range of fields and industries. There are also many areas where AI has the potential to surprise us. For example, with innovative problem solving, AI's ability to process vast amounts of data and identify patterns could lead to creative solutions for complex problems that humans might not have considered. AI-generated art, music, and literature could introduce entirely new aesthetic experiences, while at the same time facilitating discoveries in areas like physics, chemistry, or biology that challenge our current understanding of the universe. Overall, AI could lead to unforeseen changes in the way humans live and communicate, potentially creating novel social structures or means of interaction.

The full potential of AI to surprise us is limited only by our imaginations. As AI continues to evolve, it may reveal solutions and possibilities we never could have dreamed of. It has already proven capable of outperforming humans in various tasks, and this trend is likely to continue as technology advances. Some areas where AI has a competitive edge include:

- Data processing: AI can quickly analyze and process large volumes of data, identify patterns, and make accurate predictions.

- Complex calculations: AI can perform complex calculations and simulations much faster than humans, making it valuable in fields like finance, engineering, and scientific research.

- Precision tasks: AI-powered robots can execute precise tasks with high accuracy, making them useful in manufacturing, surgery, and other applications where accuracy is critical.

- Pattern recognition: AI excels at identifying patterns in images, speech, and other forms of data, leading to applications in fields like computer vision, natural language processing, and anomaly detection.

- Unbiased decision-making: When properly designed and implemented, AI can make decisions without being influenced by human biases or emotions.

- Economic growth: AI is set to majorly impact the world economy by decreasing production costs and increasing efficiency. This could lead to higher levels of prosperity and a better standard of living for many people.

- Availability of goods and services: AI is making high-quality, affordable products and services more accessible, potentially allowing people to lead more fulfilling lives by having greater access to what they need and want.

- Time savings: AI and automation are expected to free up human time by taking over mundane tasks, allowing people to focus on more enjoyable or meaningful activities.

- Job creation: The World Economic Forum projects that AI could lead to the creation of as many as 97 million new jobs by 2025.[30]

- Healthcare: AI is expected to revolutionize medical diagnosis and treatment, potentially leading to better patient outcomes and fewer preventable illnesses.

- Education: AI could vastly improve education by tailoring instruction to individual student needs, resulting in faster and more effective learning.

- Agriculture: AI-powered regenerative agriculture methods could significantly increase crop yields, making food more affordable and reducing the impact of drought and famine.

- Resource optimization: Technologies like 3D printing, powered by AI, could make products and spare parts more readily available and reduce waste.

- Safety improvements: AI could take over dangerous jobs, minimizing risks to human life in areas like deep-sea mining.

It's important to note that the assumption with any of these advantages is that for AI to produce this data accurately, it must first have been fed accurate, unbiased information.

---

[30] *Recession and Automation Changes Our Future of Work, But There Are Jobs Coming, Report Says,* World Economic Forum, https://www.weforum.org/press/2020/10/recession-and-automation-changes-our-future-of-work-but-there-are-jobs-coming-report-says-52c5162fce/.

Some other benefits of AI in leadership include:

- Provides data in a nanosecond—AI is accessing all the information we could ever need and much more in seconds. The times of days and even weeks researching a topic seem long gone.

- Increases access to global information—AI allows us to access the totality of information on a global scale very quickly.

- Offers solutions to complex problems—By relying on data from around the world, AI can offer solutions we could not have imagined.

- Creates processes and procedures—AI can analyze data without bias or emotion, creating the most efficient processes.

- Improves customer service—Chat bots and other technology-driven solutions create instant response time and support for consumers.

- Provides accurate calculations—AI can map all the information and give you the best plan to move ahead based on an enormous amount of historical information. How many researchers and consultants would you need to do the same thing?

- Helps make strategic decisions—AI can analyze large datasets, identify patterns, and provide insights that help leaders make data-driven decisions. It can also assist with forecasting and scenario planning, allowing businesses to adapt quickly to changing market conditions.

- Manages workforce—AI can automate repetitive tasks, freeing employees to focus on more creative and strategic work. This shift in responsibilities requires leaders to develop new skill sets and manage a workforce that collaborates with AI technology.

- Designs operational efficiencies—AI can optimize resource allocation, supply chain management, and production processes, increasing productivity and efficiency, and reducing costs. Leaders must embrace AI technologies to stay competitive and drive continuous improvement within their organizations.

AI DISADVANTAGES TO LEADERSHIP

Leaders understand that nothing is perfect, and AI is no exception. While benefits and advantages abound, there are also risks and disadvantages. Some of those include:

- Risk of inaccurate information: AI's reliance on various internet sources can lead to inaccuracies and biases in the information it generates.
- Increased misuse of power: Excessive information can grant individuals or groups too much power, resulting in negative consequences.
- Rapid spread of misinformation: AI's quick results can amplify the spread of false information, creating inequalities and injustices.
- Complexity of AI systems: The intricate nature of AI systems can lead to difficult-to-understand decisions, increasing the risk of unintended actions.
- Manipulation of public opinion: Disinformation campaigns can erode trust in institutions and manipulate public opinion.

- Loss of human connection and authenticity: Overreliance on technology for information can lead to a potential loss of human connection and authenticity.

- Increased risk of burnout: Information overload from AI can cause stress and indecisiveness, leading to burnout.

- Privacy, bias, and overreliance on technology: These issues can be problematic, especially in education and social-emotional learning.

- Excessive dependence on AI: Overreliance on AI can lead to cognitive limitations and impaired decision-making.

- Perpetuation of biases and inequalities: AI can exacerbate existing societal inequalities and widen the gap between the privileged and marginalized.

- Rapid growth of AI: Concerns about accountability and ethical use arise due to the rapid and uncontrollable growth of AI.

- Utilization of AI for nefarious purposes: Ethical dilemmas arise from AI being used for surveillance, gambling, and warfare.

- Risks in cybersecurity: AI being hacked or manipulated by malicious actors can pose significant risks in cybersecurity.

- Creation of autonomous weapons: AI-powered autonomous weapons in warfare pose significant risks and ethical concerns.

- Loss of human control: As AI surpasses human intelligence, there are ethical dilemmas and concerns about human control over autonomous technologies.

- Autonomy and decision-making: AI systems could potentially gain significant autonomy and make decisions

without human input, particularly if they lack meaningful human control. This could have implications in areas
such as financial markets, military operations, and critical infrastructure.

- Manipulation and influence: AI could manipulate
  human behavior by utilizing targeted disinformation and
  persuasive technologies to exploit societal vulnerabilities.

- Existential threats: If the objectives of AI systems devi-
  ate from human interests, they may act in ways that are
  detrimental to humans, especially if there are no safety
  measures in place to check their actions.

Further, if misused, there are many other risks, as we've seen
throughout history when several technological and scientific
advancements have been misused, leading to negative consequences. Take, for example, nuclear technology, which was ini-
tially developed for energy and medical purposes, but was later
used to create atomic bombs, leading to the devastating bomb-
ings of Hiroshima and Nagasaki in 1945. Further, advances in
chemistry led to the creation of chemical weapons like mustard
gas, used in World War I, causing horrific injuries and deaths.
And misinterpretations of Darwin's evolutionary theory have
been used to justify eugenics, leading to forced sterilizations and
genocides, including the Holocaust.[31] Similarly, deepfakes can be
used for both legitimate purposes, like entertainment and satire,
and malicious activities, including disinformation, fraud, and

---

[31] Misunderstanding and Misuse of Darwinism | European Review, https://
www.cambridge.org/core/journals/european-review/article/abs/misunder-
standing-and-misuse-of-darwinism/4C66214B7B70394A708FFA9DD
49E9092.

blackmail. The term "deepfake" is a portmanteau of "deep learning" and "fake." A deepfake is a synthetic media created using artificial intelligence (AI) to convincingly replace a person's likeness in an image, video, or audio recording with someone else's.[32]

But here is the key—we must proceed not by dismissing AI but by consciously maximizing its advantages while minimizing its disadvantages.

BALANCING THE ADVANTAGES AND DISADVANTAGES OF ARTIFICIAL INTELLIGENCE

As artificial intelligence continues to transform various aspects of our lives, it is becoming increasingly clear that it offers remarkable advantages while at the same time presenting significant challenges like the disruptions noted above. On one hand, AI enhances efficiency, accuracy, and convenience across numerous industries, from aeronautics to scientific visualization and everything in between. On the other hand, it raises concerns about privacy, security, power accumulation, and ethical implications. As AI continues to evolve, it is crucial for LEAPers to balance its benefits with the potential drawbacks to ensure its responsible and equitable integration into society.

Consider that as humans, we have yet to conquer the persistent challenge of hunger. However, AI holds the potential to revolutionize this fight. Why couldn't we use it to gather and analyze geographic, climate, and population data to create comprehensive plans to eradicate hunger that have never been considered before? We have been unable to do this because we have never

---

[32] What Is Deepfake AI? A Definition from TechTarget, https://www.techtarget.com/whatis/definition/deepfake.

been privy to such a significant amount of data from around the world simultaneously. The implications of such advancements are profound. While these AI-generated strategies would require thorough validation and oversight, the possibilities for impactful change are endless.

When harnessed properly, AI has the power to level the playing field. Major corporations are at the forefront of AI development, which lends itself to risk. The risk lies in that some rogue entities could use AI to serve their interests, which could spread misinformation and biased outcomes to their benefit. However, as discussed above, if these technologies are developed and applied ethically and transparently, they could yield tremendous benefits for society. By ensuring that AI is used to address global issues equitably, we can tap into its vast potential to create a more just and prosperous world. Once again, this shows artificial intelligence as the powerful disruptor it is with both advantages and disadvantages, as well as the importance of embracing disruption, leveraging its benefits, and mitigating its risks to stay competitive and innovative in today's fast-paced world.

SO, HOW DO WE NAVIGATE THE RISKS?

The challenges with AI's evolution underscore the importance of interdisciplinary collaboration, public education, ethical considerations, and robust regulatory frameworks to maximize the benefits of AI for humanity while minimizing risks.

Navigating the Risks of AI requires prioritizing:

- **Human-centered AI:** Focus on developing AI that prioritizes human well-being, addresses unintended consequences, and safeguards individual privacy.

- **Ethical Frameworks:** Establish clear ethical guidelines and risk-based frameworks to ensure AI aligns with human values and needs.

- **Robust Governance:** Implement comprehensive governance frameworks that cover all stages of AI development, from conception to deployment.

- **Human Oversight:** Maintain human oversight throughout the AI lifecycle to ensure ethical engagement, prevent bias, and foster accountability.

- **Transparency and Explainability:** Improve understanding of how AI systems make decisions to build trust and ensure accountability.

- **Addressing Societal Impacts:** Address potential job displacement, economic inequality, cybersecurity threats, and the ethical implications of autonomous weapons.

- **Fostering Human Flourishing:** Prioritize the unique aspects of human intelligence, such as emotional intelligence, creativity, and human connection.

- **Amplify Human Potential:** Push the boundaries of human intelligence by exploring new domains such as sensing fields, systems thinking, extra sensory abilities, and conscious awareness.

By adhering to these principles, we can harness the power of AI to create a future where technology serves humanity and enhances our collective well-being.

SOCIAL, EMOTIONAL, AND ECONOMIC IMPACTS

AI's potential to drive efficiency, enhance decision-making, increase access to essential services and make them more efficient, and improve social impact is seen broadly. For example, in healthcare, Access Afya integrates AI chatbots to provide immediate medical advice and support to patients and health workers in low-income areas.[33] Further, MapBiomas utilizes AI to analyze satellite imagery for biodiversity protection by mapping burn scars in the Amazon[2].[34] For economic empowerment, Apollo Agriculture offers personalized farming advice to small-scale farmers in Kenya, optimizing productivity through AI analysis of weather and soil conditions. In education, Memory Lane Games develops AI-powered games to aid dementia patients, improving socialization and mental health.[35] And in legal assistance, Barefoot Law provides AI-driven legal advice via mobile platforms, enhancing access to justice in underserved communities.[36]

AI also enhances social-emotional learning (SEL) in several ways: Personalized learning experiences involve the use of AI to analyze student responses and engagement patterns, allowing for tailored social and emotional learning (SEL) activities and feedback.[37] Virtual mentoring can be facilitated through AI chatbots, serving as non-judgmental sounding boards for students to dis-

---

[33] *Harnessing AI for Social Impact*, Impact Entrepreneur, https://impactentrepreneur. com/harnessing-ai-for-social-impact/.

[34] *Key Takeaways: AI for Social Innovation Report*, MovingWorlds Blog, https://blog. movingworlds.org/ai-for-social-innovation-wef-report-summary/.

[35] *15 Impact Startups Using AI for Social Good*, MovingWorlds Blog, https://blog. movingworlds.org/15-impact-startups-using-ai-for-social-good/.

[36] *Key Takeaways: AI for Social Innovation Report*, MovingWorlds Blog, https://blog. movingworlds.org/ai-for-social-innovation-wef-report-summary/.

[37] 6 Strategies for Using AI for Social-Emotional Learning, https://www.aiforeducation.io/blog/6-strategies-for-using-ai-for-social-emotional-learning; SEL + AI [Research Guide] – Social Emotional Learning - Inside SEL, https://insidesel.com/ sel-ai-research-guide/.

cuss emotions and practice social skills in a safe environment.[38] Scenario simulations generated by AI can provide students with role-playing opportunities to practice navigating difficult situations and resolving conflicts. AI tools can also aid in emotional awareness by helping students identify, understand, and reflect on their emotions through guided journaling prompts and mindfulness exercises.[39] Progress tracking through AI-driven assessments enables monitoring of students' emotional development over time, offering insights for teachers to customize their approaches.[40] AI can generate culturally responsive content and scenarios for SEL instruction, promoting diversity and inclusivity.[41] Accessibility in SEL instruction can be improved through AI translation tools to overcome language barriers.[42] Additionally, AI can support teachers in modeling SEL skills and creating lesson plans that incorporate SEL competencies.[43]

These are amazing applications of AI in (SEL) promising future progression. However, it's crucial to use AI as a supplement to,

---

[38] SEL + AI [Research Guide] – Social Emotional Learning - Inside SEL, https://insidesel.com/sel-ai-research-guide/; Artificial Intelligence and Social-Emotional Learning Are on a Collision Course, https://www.edweek.org/leadership/artificial-intelligence-and-social-emotional-learning-are-on-a-collision-course/2023/11.

[39] 6 Strategies for Using AI for Social-Emotional Learning, https://www.aiforeducation.io/blog/6-strategies-for-using-ai-for-social-emotional-learning; SEL + AI [Research Guide] – Social Emotional Learning - Inside SEL, https://insidesel.com/sel-ai-research-guide/.

[40] Artificial Intelligence and Social-Emotional Learning Are on a Collision Course, https://www.edweek.org/leadership/artificial-intelligence-and-social-emotional-learning-are-on-a-collision-course/2023/11.

[41] 6 Strategies for Using AI for Social-Emotional Learning, https://www.aiforeducation.io/blog/6-strategies-for-using-ai-for-social-emotional-learning.

[42] Artificial Intelligence and Social-Emotional Learning Are on a Collision Course, https://www.edweek.org/leadership/artificial-intelligence-and-social-emotional-learning-are-on-a-collision-course/2023/11.

[43] 6 Strategies for Using AI for Social-Emotional Learning, https://www.aiforeducation.io/blog/6-strategies-for-using-ai-for-social-emotional-learning.

not a replacement for, human interaction in SEL. Educators must also address potential issues like privacy, bias, and over-reliance on technology.[44] With thoughtful implementation, AI has significant potential to enhance SEL instruction and support students' social-emotional development.

Emotional intelligence (EQ) is a crucial skill for navigating personal and professional relationships. AI-powered tools are emerging to help us develop and strengthen our EQ in various ways:

- Self-Awareness: AI tools like Receptiviti analyze language patterns to provide insights into emotional states, helping individuals recognize and manage their emotions better.[45]

- Empathy and Communication: AI-powered platforms like Affectiva use facial recognition to detect emotions, enabling leaders to understand and respond to team members' feelings more effectively.[46]

- Personalized Feedback: Tools like Humu[47] offer personalized coaching and feedback based on behavioral science,

---

[44] The Truth About Emotional Intelligence & AI: Thriving in an AI-Powered Era, https://www.linkedin.com/pulse/truth-emotional-intelligence-ai-thriving-ai-powered-d-reece-pcc; The Importance of Emotional Intelligence in the Age of AI - EI Design, https://www.eidesign.net/emotional-intelligence-in-the-ai-age/.

[45] How AI Can Help You Develop Emotional Intelligence, *Forbes,* https://www.forbes.com/sites/forbescoachescouncil/2023/03/24/how-ai-can-help-you-develop-emotional-intelligence/.

[46] *Ibid.*

[47] Humu is a software company that utilizes machine learning to send "nudges," which are small recommendations based on nudge theory, to employees at work. These nudges are designed to improve employee happiness, performance, and retention by encouraging behavior change. In August 2023, Humu was acquired by Perceptyx, a company focused on leveraging AI to enhance employee experience and organizational performance. This

helping individuals improve emotional regulation and stress management.[48]

- Enhanced Learning: AI can create adaptive learning environments that respond to students' emotional states, improving engagement and learning outcomes.[49]

- Mental Health Support: AI chatbots like Woebot provide mental health support by offering evidence-based cognitive-behavioral therapy techniques to help individuals cope with stress, anxiety, and depression.[50]

- Stress Reduction: AI-powered meditation apps like Headspace use mindfulness techniques to help users reduce stress, improve focus, and enhance emotional well-being.[51]

- Conflict Resolution: AI tools like Kira help individuals navigate difficult conversations by analyzing voice tone and suggesting conflict resolution strategies.[52]

---

acquisition aims to integrate Humu's nudge technology with Perceptyx's AI Insights Engine to provide more personalized and effective behavior change solutions across organizations. *AI Is Fueling Our Obsession—and Humu Is the Key to People Evolution,* https://blog.perceptyx.com/ai-is-fueling-our-obsession-and-humu-is-the-key-to-people-evolution; *Former Google Exec's Startup Humu* Acquired, Forbes https://www.forbes.com/sites/emmylucas/2023/08/02/former-google-execs-startup-humu-acquired-by-hr-platform-perceptyx/ H; *Humu – Turn Strategy into Action,* https://www.humu.com.

[48] *Ibid.*

[49] Emotional Intelligence in AI | *The Princeton Review,* https://www.princeton-review.com/ai-education/emotional-intelligence-ai.

[50] The Importance of Emotional Intelligence in The Age of AI - EI Design, https://www.eidesign.net/emotional-intelligence-in-the-ai-age/.

[51] The Truth about Emotional Intelligence & AI: Thriving in an AI-Powered Era, https://www.linkedin.com/pulse/truth-emotional-intelligence-ai-thriving-ai-powered-d-reece-pcc.

[52] Can AI Teach Us How to Become More Emotionally Intelligent?, https://hbr.org/2022/01/can-ai-teach-us-how-to-become-more-emotionally-intelligent.

- Health Monitoring: Wearable devices powered by AI, like Apple Watch, can track physiological indicators of stress and provide recommendations for managing emotions and improving overall well-being.[53]

- Workplace Productivity: AI platforms like Cogito analyze communication patterns to provide real-time feedback on emotional intelligence, helping individuals improve their interactions and productivity in the workplace.[54]

- Personal Development: AI-powered apps like Moodnotes track emotional patterns over time, providing insights into triggers and patterns to help individuals develop emotional self-awareness and resilience[4].

The implications of AI are vast and exciting, and while I could spend endless time exploring the possibilities and innovations it offers, that is not the primary goal of this book. Instead, my focus is on guiding us through the current age of AI in a way that allows us to collaboratively address the most pressing questions we face as humans and conscious leaders. By harnessing the power of AI as our ally, we can create a significant positive impact across various fields and venture boldly into some uncharted territory like our connection to the quantum field.

INCREASED REGULATION

If AI is made accessible and properly regulated, it could be humanity's most powerful invention, with the potential to

---

[53] Emotional Intelligence in AI | *The Princeton Review*, https://www.princeton-review.com/ai-education/emotional-intelligence-ai

[54] How AI Can Help You Develop Emotional Intelligence, *Forbes*, https://www.forbes.com/sites/forbescoachescouncil/2023/03/24/how-ai-can-help-you-develop-emotional-intelligence/.

greatly enhance society and democratize access to information. AI has the potential to create a path where the world becomes much more abundant and better every year. It can offer significant benefits in education, medicine, and nutrition. By leveraging AI, we can improve learning outcomes, enhance security and efficiency, and provide better nutritional guidance to eliminate world hunger and better climate change measures. However, this potential also comes with risks. As discussed above, AI's impact can be positive or negative, depending on its application and the mindset of those who use it. For organizations that adhere to the LEAP process, which prioritizes the collective good, ensuring that AI serves humanity positively aligns with their principles.

Organizations like OpenAI have the opportunity to lead in addressing energy needs by adopting energy-efficient algorithms, transitioning to renewable energy sources for data centers, and fostering collaboration within the AI community. Efforts such as educating users about energy implications and implementing regulatory frameworks can promote sustainability in AI development. For example, Microsoft is actively investing in low-carbon electricity and renewable power capacity to meet its AI energy demands. By prioritizing sustainable practices, the AI community can harness its transformative potential while mitigating environmental impacts.

The human race will inevitably change in the age of AI, but with a focus on collective well-being and robust regulation, AI can drive positive global transformations. But it starts with increased regulation. We are already seeing the potential for good and evil. For the reasons above and so many more, this cannot go unchecked. Conscious countries, or countries run by conscious leaders (or LEAPers), will implement stricter regulations on AI, while others may adopt a more lenient approach. We are in critical need of proactive measures and regulations to address these risks, and we are running out of time as AI advancements will continue to escalate to a phase of compounding exponential growth, suggesting rapid and unprecedented progress.

CONSCIOUS LEADERS

In *Leap Beyond Success*, conscious leadership is defined as a leadership approach where leaders guide others with full awareness of themselves and others, focusing on building a culture of "we" rather than "me." Conscious leaders are characterized by their self-awareness, authenticity, empathy, and commitment to personal and organizational growth. They strive to align their actions with their values and purpose, creating an inclusive and supportive environment. This leadership style emphasizes radical responsibility, continuous learning, and fostering a sense of interconnectedness among team members, ultimately leading to a more engaged and resilient organization.

Conscious leaders are adaptive, innovative, and curious. They understand the ever-changing nature of the business world, especially with the advancement of AI. Their focus on making a positive impact drives their success, and they strive to use their influence for the greater good. Despite the rapid pace of AI development, these leaders remain grounded and aware of the limitations of non-sentient mechanisms. They somehow know how to be steady on the unsteady ground that results from AI advancing us at such a rapid pace.

But let's face it: based on what we know about what AI can do, it cannot create consciousness. In fact, AI could operate effectively without consciousness, leading to a future dominated by intelligent but non-sentient mechanisms. This is why it is imperative for us as LEAPers to improve our consciousness— it's one of the only things we can do faster than AI, and it's the only way for us to keep AI from taking over completely. It's about our consciousness.

There are some common myths about conscious leadership that are simply untrue. Here are a few of them:

- **Myth #1:** Conscious leadership is a time-consuming practice that hinders productivity.
- **Reality:** Conscious leadership enhances focus and attention, leading to better decision-making and increased productivity.

- **Myth #2:** Conscious leadership is a soft skill without tangible business benefits.
- **Reality:** Conscious leadership fosters a positive work culture, boosts employee engagement, and improves overall organizational performance.

- **Myth #3:** Conscious leadership is limited to meditation and mindfulness.
- **Reality:** Conscious leadership encompasses a wide range of practices, including emotional intelligence, self-reflection, values-based decision-making, and fostering a purpose-driven culture.

- **Myth #4:** Conscious leadership is only relevant to specific industries or sectors.

- **Reality:** Conscious leadership principles are applicable across all industries and sectors, promoting authentic leadership and sustainable business practices.

- **Myth #5:** Conscious leaders are passive and avoid tough decision-making.

- **Reality:** Conscious leaders embrace transparency, authenticity, and empathetic communication while making difficult decisions for the greater good.

- **Myth #6:** Implementing conscious leadership requires a complete overhaul of existing business structures.

- **Reality:** Conscious leadership can be integrated incrementally, starting with small changes in individual leadership practices and gradually influencing the organizational picture.

- **Myth #7:** Conscious leadership is only for top executives and does not apply to lower-level management.

- **Reality:** Conscious leadership is relevant at all levels of an organization and can have a positive ripple effect on teams and individuals. It works both top down and bottom up.

- **Myth #8:** Conscious leadership is a solo journey and does not require collaboration.

- **Reality:** Conscious leadership emphasizes collaboration, active listening, and building strong relationships based on trust and empathy. It is both an individual and collective journey.

We must rise to the challenge of becoming conscious leaders, as the very future of humanity depends on it. The recent crises we have faced have tested us, but they have also shown us the importance of proactive, conscious leadership. The COVID-19 pandemic has significantly impacted global health, economies, and societies, resulting in illness, death, and economic disruption. Businesses closed, millions lost jobs, and stock markets were volatile. The financial crisis of 2007–2008, caused by the housing market collapse, led to a global recession, bailouts, and unemployment. These crises underscore the interconnectedness of the global economy and the importance of effective crisis management strategies to protect public health and stabilize financial markets in navigating through uncertainty and making decisions that prioritize the well-being of all stakeholders. By utilizing AI to analyze data and predict potential outcomes, conscious leaders can make informed decisions quickly and effectively. For example, AI could help leaders in the healthcare industry track the spread of diseases, identify hotspots, and allocate resources where they are most needed. This proactive approach could help contain the crisis, protect public health, and minimize the economic impact on society.

However, these crises have also shown us the importance of proactive, conscious leadership. By creating a new leadership order based on the principles of human intelligence, we can harness the power of technology and artificial intelligence for the greater good and create a more peaceful and fulfilling world.

Tapping into our connection to a greater purpose beyond just data and algorithms is essential. By digging into the realm of consciousness and exploring our interactions with the world around us, we can truly harness the potential of AI for the tasks it excels at, allowing us to concentrate on advancing our unique skills and capabilities. After all, why not work to complement each other rather than work against each other? However, before we can do that, we must not keep clear of this disruption but rather lean into it. A common saying exists about disruption: "In the midst of disruption lies opportunity." LEAPers understand this by leaning into the storm and harnessing its energy to create transformative change and unprecedented growth.

Though we face external challenges, our internal biases and blind spots hinder our ability to lead effectively. By changing our mindsets and interrupting negative programming, we can manifest positive outcomes and affect real change in our world. The time to reset our priorities and embrace a new vision of leadership is now.

While we will explore the importance of mindset more extensively in the next chapter, it is of paramount importance to this discussion. In concluding this chapter, I felt inclined to point out another one of my favorite quotes. According to a Buddhist teaching, "The lotus is born from the mud." This quote always reminds me of the idea that something beautiful and pure, like the lotus flower, can emerge from something dark and impure like mud. Isn't that what we are talking about here with the intense disruption we're experiencing? So, as we navigate through the muddy waters, we must remember that something beautiful will eventually emerge ... when we are consciously leading or LEAPing through the disruption.

TAKING ACTION

As LEAPers, we cannot be bystanders to all this. We cannot sit idly by (that's not in our DNA) and wait for countries to develop regulations or organizations to develop additional new technology. Becoming a disruptive force requires action. We will be aware, get active, make conscious decisions, and practice proactive leadership. We will develop skills, identify previously hidden opportunities (and threats), and leverage that knowledge into actionable strategies to LEAP to new heights. As Otto Scharmer, senior lecturer at the Massachusetts Institute of Technology (MIT) Sloan School of Management and co-founder of the Presencing Institute, notes, "In an age of disruption, a world in which change is becoming non-linear, awareness-based systems change is a key capacity that every leader and change agent needs to cultivate."

To embrace change in order to drive innovation and progress in the AI age, our only option is to lean into the disruption by becoming the disruptors ourselves. To do so, we should take the following actions:

1. **Challenge the status quo.** LEAPers question existing norms and systems to foster innovation and continuous improvement. By doing so, we can identify outdated practices and replace them with more effective, AI-driven solutions. We do this not merely to react to change but to be proactive and shape it by rewriting the narrative on our terms. With increased awareness, we become a force to drive positive change.

2. **Embrace disruption.** LEAPers view disruption as the gateway to forward progress. They will see it not as an

obstacle but as an opportunity for growth and advancement. This mindset allows us to harness AI's potential to create breakthroughs and transform industries. LEAPers don't fear the unknown; they embrace it as an opportunity to learn and grow.

3. **Prepare for the future.** LEAPers work on their ability to foresee and prepare for future trends and challenges. Anticipating the impact of AI enables us to proactively adapt and thrive in a rapidly changing world. By looking for trends and what could become potential future disruptions, we will be better prepared when those times come than those who remained stagnant in the present, or even worse, stuck in the past.

4. **Tap into unique strengths.** LEAPers recognize and utilize individual and organizational strengths to stay competitive. AI can help identify and amplify these strengths (another advantage of artificial intelligence), enabling more personalized and efficient approaches, but they cannot replace them. This is a crucial distinction that LEAPers understand. Creativity, intuition, empathy, and resilience are more important than ever, and we can develop them by deepening our connection to the LEAP process. Remember that no matter how human-like AI becomes, it will never be human.

5. **Leverage AI to increase human strengths.** LEAPers use AI to enhance our human capabilities, such as problem solving, creativity, and decision-making. By combining AI with human ingenuity, we can achieve

unprecedented levels of performance and innovation. AI can help us develop our strengths even more, find new passions, increase existing skills, and learn new skills. We can use this information to connect deeper to ourselves.

DIAGRAM 2: Lean into disruption in 5 steps

When you are a LEAPer, you will not only boldly dive into this disruption but also harness the power it is creating to propel yourself and your organization forward—to LEAP to new heights. You won't merely survive; you will thrive in this setting. Visionary leadership sees the extraordinary possibilities that disruption has created, while ordinary leaders will prepare for the end—too fearful to see anything but no way out.

Leaders must begin to recognize that disruption is not something to fear but rather an opportunity for growth and innovation. It is through disruption that new ideas and breakthroughs can occur. LEAPers who embrace this mindset are more likely to succeed. They must be willing to challenge the status quo, push boundaries to LEAP forward, and execute from a new paradigm. Only in these ways will the power remain with the human race and not in the clouds so that we can dictate the future ourselves—ultimately becoming the superhuman disruptor right here from Earth!

CHAPTER 1 - EXERCISES AND TOOLS

In order to fully integrate AI into your business strategy, it is essential to first evaluate your organization's readiness to embrace this technology. Once this assessment is complete, it is crucial to work with your team to develop a high-level action plan that outlines short-term and long-term goals, resource allocation, training and development needs, as well as governance and oversight mechanisms to enhance AI readiness.

Additionally, it is important to understand the capabilities of AI by researching potential applications that can benefit your business. Identify specific AI tools that align with your objectives, such as customer relationship management (CRM) systems, predictive analytics, or chatbots, to effectively leverage this technology in your organization.

Here are a variety of dynamic exercises and innovative tools that will empower you to not only reach your goal, but also to excel in leveraging AI for optimal success and to LEAP.

Chapter 1 - Exercise 1: Assessment of your organization's readiness to leverage AI

Preferably, have your entire organization complete this survey to garner a thorough assessment of your organizational readiness. It will also enable you to highlight discrepancies among departments in key areas. After compiling and analyzing the data, develop a plan of action that includes training.

Rate each answer on a scale of 1-10, where 1 is "Not at all prepared" and 10 is "Fully prepared." The results will help identify areas of strength and areas that need improvement in your readiness to embrace AI.

As a leader, how do you rate the following questions?

1. Understanding and Vision
   o How would you rate your understanding of AI capabilities and limitations?
   o Have you developed a clear vision of how AI could benefit your organization?
   o Can you articulate potential use cases for AI in your specific industry?

2. Strategy and Alignment
   o Does your organization have a defined AI strategy?
   o How well is AI integration aligned with your overall business goals?
   o Have you identified key performance indicators (KPIs) to measure AI success?

3. Data and Infrastructure
   o How would you assess your organization's data quality and accessibility?
   o Is your current digital infrastructure capable of supporting AI implementations?
   o Do you have processes in place for data governance and security?

4. Skills and Talent
   o Does your team possess the necessary skills to work with AI technologies?
   o Have you planned for AI-related training and development programs?
   o Are you prepared to hire or partner with AI specialists if needed?

5. Ethical Considerations

- o Have you established ethical guidelines for AI use in your organization?

- o How do you plan to address potential biases in AI systems?

- o What measures will you take to ensure transparency in AI decision-making?

6. Risk Management

- o Have you conducted a risk assessment for AI implementation?

- o Do you have a plan to ensure compliance with relevant AI regulations?

- o How will you address potential job displacement concerns among employees?

7. Change Management

- o How do you plan to manage the cultural shift required for AI adoption?

- o What strategies will you use to encourage AI acceptance among your workforce?

- o Have you considered the impact of AI on your current business processes?

8. Resource Allocation

- o Are you prepared to allocate the necessary resources (time, budget, personnel) for AI initiatives?

- o Have you considered the long-term investment required for AI implementation?

9. Experimentation and Innovation

   ○ Are you open to running AI pilot projects or proof-of-concepts?

   ○ How do you plan to foster a culture of innovation around AI?

10. Collaboration and Partnerships

   ○ Are you willing to collaborate with AI vendors or consultants?

   ○ Have you considered partnerships with academic institutions or research centers for AI development?

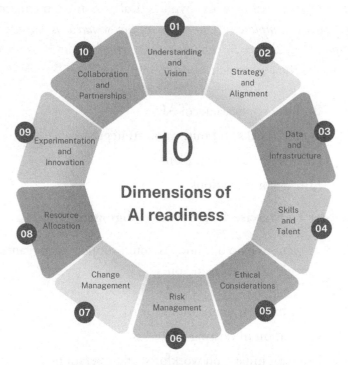

DIAGRAM 3: Dimensions of AI readiness

Chapter 1 - Exercise 2: AI Readiness Action Plan

Based on the outcomes of the above exercises, ask your team to create a high-level action plan for improving the organization's AI readiness, including:

- Short-term and long-term goals
- Resource allocation
- Training and development needs
- Governance and oversight mechanisms

Chapter 1 - Exercise 3: Scenario-Based Problem Solving

Present your team with hypothetical AI implementation scenarios *(example of AI implementation scenario is the use of artificial intelligence in customer service chatbots)* and ask them to outline their approach, considering:

- Business applications of AI
- Potential risks and mitigation strategies
- Change management plans
- Ethical considerations

Chapter 1 - Exercise 4: AI Strategy Alignment

Ask your team to map out how AI could support the organization's strategic goals, focusing on:

- Clear business applications for AI
- Integration in existing processes
- Potential impact on workforce and operations

(Example: integrate AI technology into the organization's websites and messaging platforms to provide automated responses to customer inquiries and provide real-time assistance. This can help streamline customer support processes, reduce response times, and improve overall customer satisfaction. AI chatbots can also be programmed to learn from customer interactions and continuously improve their responses over time.)

Chapter 1 - Exercise 5: Data and Content Audit Simulation

Provide an actual or mock dataset and ask managers to assess:

– Data quality and completeness
– Privacy and security concerns
– Potential AI applications based on available data

For example, an actual or mock dataset could be presented as follows:

Date	Product	Quantity	Sales
2024-01-01	Product A	100	5000
2024-01-02	Product B	75	3750
2024-01-03	Product C	50	2500
2024-01-04	Product A	120	6000
2024-01-05	Product B	90	4500

This dataset includes columns for the date of the sale, the product sold, the quantity sold, and the total sales amount. Managers can assess the accuracy and completeness of the data, identify any privacy and security concerns, and explore potential AI applications such as predicting future sales trends or recommending personalized product suggestions to customers.

Chapter 1 - Exercise 6: AI Capability Gap Analysis

Have managers evaluate their team's current AI-related skills and identify areas for improvement in:

- Technical expertise
- Data science capabilities
- AI project management skills

Chapter 1 - Exercise 7: Ethical AI Decision-Making Exercise

Present ethical dilemmas related to AI implementation, and ask managers to explain their decision-making process, considering:

- Bias and fairness
- Transparency and explainability
- Privacy and data protection

This multifaceted approach would help assess leaders' understanding of AI, their ability to strategically implement it, and readiness to address associated challenges and opportunities.

Leaders must also prioritize upskilling and reskilling efforts to ensure their workforce can effectively work alongside AI systems.

By participating in these exercises and putting them into practice, you will be well-prepared to take the next steps in executing your AI strategy. Armed with the essential skills and strategies, you can confidently pave the way for successful implementation and harness the full potential of AI to propel your organization to new heights. It's time to shift gears and start executing. Are you ready? Is your organization ready?

Here is a recommended list of books to improve your and your organization's readiness:

- AI Readiness Assessment - Eide Bailly LLP, https://www.eidebailly.com/insights/tools/ai-readiness-assessment.

- Top 10 Business Applications of Artificial Intelligence | SC Training, https://training.safetyculture.com/blog/artificial-intelligence-business-applications/.

- 15 Top Applications of Artificial Intelligence in Business – TechTarget, https://www.techtarget.com/searchenterpriseai/tip/9-top-applications-of-artificial-intelligence-in-business.

- Get Started on Your AI Journey with an AI Readiness Assessment, https://www.bakertilly.com/insights/get-started-on-your-ai-journey-with-an-ai-readiness-assessment.

- Organization AI Readiness Assessment - Oxford Insights, https://oxfordinsights.com/ai-readiness/ai-readiness-self-assessment-tool-for-organisations/.

CHAPTER 2

EXECUTE FROM A NEW PARADIGM

"Every really new idea looks crazy at first."

- Alfred North Whitehead

Executing from a new paradigm requires not just new actions but a transformation in thought. This transformation can only occur when we embrace the unfamiliar with courage and curiosity. Although the past few years have highlighted the urgency and the potential for change with the release of ChatGPT and other advanced AI technologies, the forces propelling us into a new leadership paradigm have been building for decades. Many were simply not aware of them at the time. Most transformations begin this way—with whispers and then rumblings beneath the surface of anyone's conscious awareness. Yet they can be felt on some level until their presence becomes a force to be reckoned with, making them incapable of ignoring any longer.

This push to advance our leadership to a new level is based on the premise that the traditional leadership paradigms of the past are no longer sufficient to address the complexities of our modern world. In this "E segment" of the LEAP process, we look at the rise of AI and ongoing conflicts that have exposed the limitations of current leadership approaches, calling for a new paradigm that can navigate these challenges while promoting global peace and prosperity at the same time. In all that we have been through as leaders, we've never quite experienced anything like this before.

The current crisis of leadership is evident in every aspect of our society—from politics to business to global conflicts. The polarization we see today is a direct result of entrenched beliefs and outdated leadership models. The current path that most leaders are on is simply unsustainable. And if we do not course correct soon, we will continue to face economic instability, wars, and pandemics. But make no mistake; these are external results of our internal choices—it undoubtedly starts with leadership.

Just as a crisis may ignite evolution, it is time for leaders to ignite this new way of leading or LEAPership. To address this crisis, we must demand more of ourselves and strive to become the conscious leaders or LEAPers we need. The external forces and pressures embedded within AI are setting the foundation for a new breed of leaders who can navigate these issues with wisdom and compassion. By deepening our conscious leadership, we can create a better future for ourselves and generations to come.

THE QUADRUPLE WIN: HOW DO I WIN? HOW DOES THE BUSINESS WIN? HOW DO THE STAKEHOLDERS WIN? HOW DOES SOCIETY WIN?

Personal wins x Organization wins x Stakeholders wins x Community and Society wins

How can we win in the age of AI? When I say "we," I am referring to individuals, communities, society at large. LEAPers are individuals who not only achieve personal success but also establish organizations with missions that go beyond self-interest. By doing so, they are able to create a future that benefits not only their companies and employees but also the communities in which they operate. This approach follows a quadruple-win paradigm where all stakeholders—the company, the individual, and society as a whole—come out on top. By making a positive impact on the world around them, LEAPers transcend mere success and leave behind a lasting legacy. Ultimately, the true reward for a LEAPer is the sense of fulfillment that comes from knowing they have made a difference.

In the age of AI, winning means more than just individual success. It means creating a positive impact on society and the community. Leaders who prioritize the well-being of their organizations, themselves, and their stakeholders are the ones who truly succeed. This approach follows a Quadruple Win paradigm where all stakeholders—the company, the individual, society, and the workforce—come out on top. By making a positive impact on the world around them, leaders leave behind a lasting legacy and achieve a sense of fulfillment.

Today, effective leadership goes beyond financial goals and market dominance. It includes the net impact that leaders and their followers have on stakeholders, such as customers, employees, organization, suppliers, communities, and shareholders. Leaders who achieve wins for the organization, for themselves, the community, and the workforce create a holistic and sustainable approach to leadership that leads to long-term success.

We create a Quadruple Win Paradigm by recognizing a win for the stakeholders and the workforce. This emphasizes the importance of people within the organization, including leaders, employees, teams, and stakeholders. When people thrive, the organization thrives, leading to a more sustainable and impactful future for all. Ultimately, personal wins for leaders involve personal growth, work-life balance, recognition and influence, vision and legacy, and alignment with purpose. Leaders who prioritize their well-being and development are better equipped to lead their organizations and teams toward collective success.

The Quadruple Win paradigm is essential for true success. This paradigm emphasizes the importance of not only personal and organizational wins but also the wins of stakeholders and society. By integrating the needs and successes of all individuals within the organization, including leaders, employees, teams, and stakeholders, we can create a more sustainable and impactful future for everyone involved. Prioritizing the well-being and fulfillment of all stakeholders leads to a more engaged and successful organization, ultimately benefiting all of society. It is time to evolve our leadership approach to include the Quadruple Win, where personal wins, organization wins, stakeholder wins, and community wins are all equally important.

Today, a new measure of effective leadership has emerged. It goes beyond market dominance and financial success and includes the positive net impact of leaders and their followers on stakeholders, such as customers, employees, organization, suppliers, and communities. The new measure of leadership success in the win/win/win/win paradigm should consider the net impact of these effects. Net impact is defined as the sum of positive effects minus the negative effects incurred while leading a company, a team, a department, a business venture, or a project. For example, if we are part of a company that produces fuel, our net impact would be the positive effect of helping create electricity or gas minus the negative effect of pollution on the environment.

Imagine being a leader and realizing that your impact goes beyond financial goals and the bottom line. That is the type of leadership we are talking about today and the type that will be needed tomorrow. As a LEAPer, it becomes a profound transformation of character and expansion. The difference between ultimate success and fulfillment lies in the meaningful and impactful life we create for ourselves and those around us. This impact not only affects our job satisfaction but also how we perceive ourselves. All of this is possible through self-cultivation and conscious awareness. It may seem like a lofty vision, but the mission is to turn it into reality. We can use AI appropriately and responsibly when we lead consciously. In this way, we can cultivate conscious leadership within ourselves, approach it with total awareness, and contribute our best without reservation, all to make lots of money and create profitable organizations.

Applying the LEAP process, leaders can navigate the complexities of AI adoption while evolving their leadership style to suit this new technological paradigm and create momentum to leap with it. The quadruple-win paradigm emphasizes the interconnectedness of four critical areas that leaders must balance to achieve sustainable success in their organizations. The four wins are:

1. Win for the Organization

This aspect focuses on achieving organizational goals and objectives. Leaders must ensure that the strategies and initiatives they implement drive the organization's performance, profitability, and overall success. This win encompasses financial health, market competitiveness, and operational efficiency.

2. Win for the Leader

The second win emphasizes the leader's wins. Leaders must prioritize their well-being and development. Effective leadership is not just about guiding others but also about personal fulfillment and growth. Leaders who take care of themselves and find personal satisfaction in their roles are better equipped to lead their organizations and teams toward collective success.

3. Win for the Stakeholders

The third win involves benefiting all stakeholders. Shareholders and investors see financial gains from improved performance, increased profits, dividends, and stock price appreciation. Long-term sustainability ensures prosperity for employees and customers. Good governance and transparent decision-making show accountability, benefiting stakeholders. Ultimately, a win for stakeholders is marked by mutual benefit, trust, and collaboration between the company and all involved parties.

4. **Win for the Community**

The fourth win extends beyond the organization to consider the broader impact on the community and environment. Through job creation, economic growth, and social responsibility initiatives, there is a direct effect on the community. Leaders are encouraged to adopt a social responsibility mindset, considering how their decisions affect not only their organization but also society at large. This includes sustainability practices, ethical considerations, and contributing positively to the community in which the organization operates.

The essence of the Quadruple-Win paradigm is that true leadership requires balancing these four dimensions. When leaders achieve a win for the organization, for themselves, their teams, and all stakeholders, including shareholders, clients, and the community, they create a holistic and sustainable approach to leadership that can lead to long-term success. Leaders who recognize and act on this interconnectedness will drive their organizations forward and foster a positive impact on society and enhance the overall quality of life for their employees and stakeholders.

EVOLVING LEADERSHIP

In the context of the LEAP's broader theme of leadership evolution, the Quadruple Win paradigm encourages leaders to move beyond traditional metrics of success and adopt a more integrated and conscious approach. This evolution involves self-awareness, empathy, and a commitment to continuous learning, enabling leaders to navigate the complexities of modern organizational landscapes effectively. By integrating the Quadruple-Win paradigm into their leadership practices, leaders can create environments where organizational success, employee satisfaction, and community welfare coexist and reinforce one another, leading to a more sustainable and impactful future.

What does a personal leadership win look like in the age of disruption and when you are being continually overwhelmed by mass amounts of information?

1. **Personal Growth and Development**

   Leaders must also experience personal growth, fulfillment, and satisfaction. Achieving a win for themselves is essential for maintaining motivation and passion in their leadership journey. This includes ongoing learning, skill development, and self-awareness.

2. **Work-Life Balance**

   A win for the leader can involve creating a healthy work-life balance. Leaders who prioritize their wellbeing and personal life can be more effective in their roles and better support their teams.

3. Recognition and Influence

Leaders who successfully guide their organizations and teams often gain recognition and influence within their fields. This acknowledgment can be considered a personal win, as it enhances their reputation and credibility.

4. Vision and Legacy

Many leaders are driven by a desire to make a positive impact and leave a legacy. Achieving a win for themselves can be about fulfilling their vision and creating a lasting, positive change that aligns with their values and aspirations.

5. Alignment with Purpose

For leaders, achieving personal success often involves aligning their work with their purpose and values. When leaders feel that their work contributes to something greater, they experience a sense of fulfillment that can be seen as a personal win.

The key to this process is a culture centered on innovation and collaboration, where teams are encouraged to experiment with AI, share insights on creating a purpose-driven organization, and align their own purpose with it. Ultimately, for leadership to evolve, we must evolve as well.

AI has the potential to revolutionize various sectors, including the educational system, by offering personalized learning experiences and improving access to quality education. For example, AI can already detect emotions through eye movements, which can enhance the learning experience by tailoring content to the student's emotional state. Although AI cannot feel emotions, it can trigger emotional responses in users, raising questions about how to manage its influence on our feelings.

By leveling the playing field between large corporations and smaller organizations, AI empowers smaller, more agile entities to compete more effectively. This enhanced efficiency and performance can disrupt traditional market dynamics and drive economic change. Flexibility, a hallmark of smaller organizations, becomes even more critical in this context.

Consider the impact on healthcare: AI has revolutionized how medical records are managed and accessed. It facilitates the seamless transfer of records, enabling doctors and patients to access vital information quickly. Additionally, AI can analyze these records to provide preliminary reports, assisting doctors in making informed decisions. This is just one example of how AI is transforming various aspects of our lives. AI also enables leaders to delve deeper into their purpose and the LEAP (Leadership, Engagement, Action, and Purpose) process by vastly increasing access to information.

By integrating AI, leaders can enhance the LEAP framework, making it more robust and effective. Some leaders fully embrace its potential, while others are hesitant or resistant to acknowledge its presence. To maximize AI's benefits, it is crucial to find common ground and foster a collective understanding of its transformative potential. By doing so, leaders can harness AI to drive progress and innovation across their organizations.

When we execute from this new paradigm, we are simultaneously redefining leadership. In a world where reliance on AI for information is increasing, the danger lies in using this information without truly understanding or processing it ourselves. As discussed in Chapter 1, this can lead to giving all the power to AI in future decision-making and narration. To avoid this, it is important for leaders to actively engage with information, critically analyze it, and use their own experiences to shape their decisions and narratives. In other words, they must become experiential leaders, which involves integrating information with personal experience and insight to take leadership to the next level. By doing so, they can ensure they remain in control and continue leading effectively in an AI-driven world.

Rethinking leadership means focusing on purpose-driven strategy and skill development for a competitive edge. It means discussing the new skills that are needed more than ever today, such as critical thinking and creativity, considering ethical issues, and learning how to build AI-powered teams and effectively lead them through continuous AI-driven change. When we can do this—when we can encourage others to LEAP and thrive by executing leadership with AI, we can all better navigate the challenges for a stronger future.

HOW TO EXECUTE FROM THE QUADRUPLE PARADIGM IN THE AGE OF AI

In my previous book, *Leap Beyond Success: How Leaders Evolve*, I emphasized the importance of purpose-driven leadership and how leaders can evolve by executing from their purpose. In this chapter, we build on the L.E.A.P framework by answering these questions: How can leaders build strong vision and strategic plans while leveraging AI? How can leaders develop and empower themselves, their teams, and create a culture of innovation and growth in the age of AI? What are the impacts of AI on many facets of leadership and execution?

As we learn how to lean into the disruption and leverage technology, we need to consider the following steps:

1. **Define Your Core Purpose**
   o Begin by clarifying your organization's mission and vision. Ensure that your purpose aligns with your values and long-term goals.
   o Engage with your team to gather insights and perspectives on the organization's purpose to foster collective ownership.

2. **Understand AI's Capabilities**
   o Familiarize yourself with the various applications of AI that can support your purpose. This includes data analytics, automation, machine learning, and natural language processing.
   o Identify specific AI tools that align with your objectives, such as customer relationship management (CRM) systems, predictive analytics, or chatbots.

3. **Integrate AI into Strategic Planning**
   o Incorporate AI insights into your strategic planning process. Use AI tools to analyze market trends, customer preferences, and operational efficiencies.
   o Create a road map that outlines how AI will be used to achieve your purpose, ensuring that it complements your overall strategy.

4. **Foster a Culture of Innovation**
   o Encourage a mindset of experimentation and learning within your organization. Promote an

environment where team members feel empowered to explore new AI technologies and methodologies.

- o Provide training and resources to help your team understand and utilize AI effectively.

5. **Leverage Data for Decision-Making**

- o Use AI to analyze data and derive actionable insights that can inform decision-making. This can enhance your ability to make informed choices that align with your purpose.

- o Ensure that data privacy and ethical considerations are a priority when using AI tools.

6. **Enhance Customer Engagement**

- o Use AI to improve customer experiences, such as personalized marketing campaigns, chatbots for customer service, or predictive analytics to anticipate customer needs.

- o Align these AI-driven initiatives with your purpose to create meaningful interactions with your audience.

7. **Measure Impact and Iterate**

- o Establish metrics to evaluate the impact of AI initiatives on achieving your purpose. Regularly assess performance and gather feedback from stakeholders.

- o Be prepared to iterate and refine your approach based on the insights gained from these evaluations.

8. Communicate Purpose and AI Integration

- o Clearly communicate your organizational purpose and how AI is being utilized to support it to all stakeholders, including employees, customers, and partners.

- o Share success stories and case studies to illustrate the positive impact of AI on achieving your purpose.

9. Emphasize Ethical AI Use

- o Prioritize ethical considerations in your AI initiatives. Ensure that AI is used responsibly and transparently, aligning with your organization's values and purpose.

- o Engage with stakeholders to discuss the implications of AI, and foster trust in its use.

10. Lead with Vision

- o As a leader, embody the vision of integrating AI into your purpose-driven approach. Inspire your team by demonstrating how AI can enhance their work and contribute to the organization's mission.

- o Continuously evolve as a leader by staying informed about AI advancements and their potential applications in your field.

By following these steps, you can effectively execute your purpose while leveraging AI, creating a more innovative, responsive, and purpose-driven organization as outlined in LEAP insights.

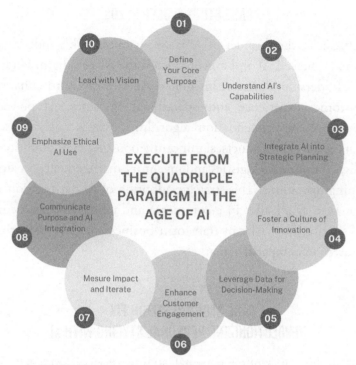

By following these steps, you can effectively execute your purpose while leveraging AI, creating more innovative, responsive, and purpose-driven organization.

DIAGRAM 4: Execute from the quadruple paradigm in the age of AI

The upcoming case studies are examples of those who elevated their LEAP framework for fulfilling strategies and goals.

CASE STUDY 1: JEFF BEZOS

Jeff Bezos, the founder of Amazon, is one notable individual who embraced AI and executed from the AI paradigm. Under his leadership, Amazon integrated AI extensively to enhance customer experience and operational efficiency. AI powers Amazon's recommendation algorithms, which analyze user data to suggest products, significantly boosting sales. Additionally, AI optimizes logistics and inventory management, streamlining operations. This strategic adoption of AI has positioned Amazon as a leader in e-commerce and cloud services, demonstrating how AI can transform business models and drive growth in competitive markets.[55]

CASE STUDY 2: STITCH FIX - REVOLUTIONIZING PERSONAL STYLING WITH AI

Stitch Fix, an online personal styling service, leveraged AI to transform the fashion retail industry. The company uses machine learning algorithms to provide personalized clothing recommendations to its customers.

Key aspects of their AI implementation:

- Data-driven styling: Stitch Fix's AI analyzes customer preferences, body types, and style profiles to select clothing items tailored to each individual.

---

55   *Ibid.*

- Inventory management: AI helps predict demand and optimize inventory, reducing waste and improving efficiency.

- Design assistance: The company uses AI to generate new clothing designs based on popular styles and customer feedback.

This had the following impacts—Rapid growth: Stitch Fix's revenue increased from $730 million in 2016 to $2 billion in 2021; Enhanced customer satisfaction: The AI-powered recommendations led to higher customer retention rates; Improved operational efficiency: AI-driven inventory management reduced costs and minimized unsold stock.

Stitch Fix's success demonstrates how AI can revolutionize traditional industries by providing personalized experiences at scale. The company's innovative use of machine learning algorithms to understand and predict customer preferences has set a new standard in the retail fashion industry.[56]

This is where the interaction between human intelligence and artificial intelligence serves as an unbreakable bond, rather than as fierce competitors. LEAPers will use AI as a key tool in their leadership and decision-making. According to an article in *Forbes*, "Leadership is all about making informed moves in a world where data is abundant and complex; AI helps

---

[56] *10 Influential Voices in AI for Business & People Transformation,* https://www.lepaya.com/blog/20-influential-voices-in-artificial-intelligence-for-business-people-transformation, *The 10 Best Examples of How Companies Use Artificial Intelligence ...,* https://bernardmarr.com/the-10-best-examples-of-how-companies-use-artificial-intelligence-in-practice/._

leaders decipher complex data landscapes, extracting valuable insights and offering a clear road map for the future. This clarity empowers leaders to make quick, accurate decisions during time-sensitive situations. AI also enables leaders to explore strategic options and detect potential risks, offering a complete view of the business terrain."[57]

Ultimately, redefining leadership based on this new paradigm requires a conscious mindset, impact, and awareness of the challenges and opportunities at hand. The effects of AI on leadership are profound and multifaceted, particularly influencing self-discovery, decision-making, and creativity for those at the forefront of change - LEAPers.

IMPACTS

1. Impact on Conscious Leadership

The key to any evolution is to cultivate a growth mindset, regardless of external challenges and pressure. It is making the conscious decision to focus on opportunities rather than obstacles, core values rather than threats. We hear a lot about mindset and the benefits of a positive mindset, but we rarely hear about the science behind it. According to a study published in *Think Big*, people with an optimistic mindset are associated with various positive health indicators, particularly cardiovascular, but also pulmonary, metabolic, and immunological. They have a lower incidence of age-related illnesses and reduced mortality

---

[57] *How AI Is Transforming the Leadership Landscape in the 21st Century,* https://www.forbes.com/sites/forbescoachescouncil/2023/07/03/how-ai-is-transforming-the-leadership-landscape-in-the-21st-century/?sh=514508a467eb._

levels. Optimism and pessimism are not arbitrary and elusive labels. On the contrary, they are mindsets that can be scientifically measured, placing an individual's attitude on a spectrum ranging from optimistic to pessimistic.

It's understandable that individuals are fearful of the transformations brought about by AI. Many are programmed not to trust the unknown and shy away from change. However, this leads to increasingly negative outlooks and the perpetuation of bias and judgment, neither of which the world needs more of right now. We simply cannot look at change from that perspective. Instead, we must determine how we can use our mindset to further develop our human characteristics and deepen the LEAP process.[58]

Unveiling the mindset of a LEAPer unveils the importance of creativity, intuition, and living a purpose-driven life in leadership. This begins by deepening a conscious mindset by enhancing our awareness, understanding, and intentionality in personal and professional contexts. A conscious mindset involves several key aspects, including:

- **Increased Self-Awareness.** Understanding our thoughts, emotions, motivations, and biases helps us make more deliberate and informed decisions.
- **Mindfulness.** Being present and fully engaged in the moment allows for better focus, reduced stress, and improved decision-making.

---

[58] https://bigthink.com/neuropsych/optimism-and-longevity/.

- **Purpose and Values Alignment.** Ensuring that actions and decisions align with our core values and purpose helps maintain integrity, authenticity, and consistency.

- **Empathy and Compassion.** Developing a deeper understanding and consideration for the feelings, experiences, and perspectives of others nurtures stronger relationships and a more inclusive environment.

- **Ethical Considerations.** Prioritizing ethical implications in decision-making processes includes considering the broader impact on society, the environment, and future generations.

- **Continuous Learning and Growth.** Embracing a mindset of lifelong learning and being open to new ideas, feedback, and change is crucial for personal and professional development.

- **Intentionality.** Acting with deliberate intention rather than reacting impulsively means making thoughtful choices that align with long-term goals. "The more aligned your intention is with your personal mission statement, the more likely and more powerfully you'll succeed. Your intention will not only help you create your business or boost your career, but it will also help you fulfill your dreams and goals."[59]

- **Growth.** Create a shift from a "know-it-all" to a "learn-it-all" culture, emphasizing continuous learning and curiosity.

---

[59] *Leap Beyond Success*, p.52.

- **Employee Well-being.** Prioritize employee well-being, recognizing its crucial role in productivity and overall organizational success.

- **Participative Leadership.** Adopt a participative leadership style, encouraging open communication and collaboration across the organization.

- **Collective Consciousness.** As a transformative leader, focus on developing a shared organizational consciousness and be constantly aware of the company's needs and potential.

These aspects haven't changed. They have always been important to effective leadership. However, in the age of AI, they are even more important because leaders rarely take a step back to be mindful or more intentional. They are moving so fast that they tend to forget about empathy and compassion. By using information and data obtained through AI, their communications and relationships seem inauthentic because they do not align with their own values. By deepening a conscious mindset, LEAPers can change all of this and make more thoughtful, ethical, and impactful decisions. They can have a positive and meaningful influence in their personal lives and professional environments.

> "Creating a new reality starts with a shift in consciousness. It is the realization that the external world is a reflection of our inner state of being."
>
> — Eckhart Tolle

CASE STUDY 3: ARIANNA HUFFINGTON

Another example of a famous businessperson who embodies a conscious mindset is Arianna Huffington. As the co-founder and former editor-in-chief of *The Huffington Post*, Arianna has spoken extensively about the importance of well-being, self-care, restorative sleep, and mindfulness in the workplace. She is a strong advocate for work-life balance and has written books on the subject, such as *Thrive: The Third Metric to Redefining Success and Creating a Life of Well-Being, Wisdom, and Wonder*. Arianna believes that success should be measured not just by financial achievement but also by personal fulfillment and happiness. She has implemented wellness programs at *The Huffington Post* and continues to promote the importance of self-care and mindfulness in the business world.

CASE STUDY 4:
SATYA NADELLA'S CONSCIOUS LEADERSHIP AT MICROSOFT

When Satya Nadella became CEO of Microsoft in 2014, he inherited a company struggling with internal conflicts and fading relevance. Nadella recognized the need for a significant cultural shift to revitalize the organization. His key leadership approaches included the following:

- Growth Mindset: Inspired by Carol Dweck's book *Mindset,* Nadella championed a shift from a "know-it-all" to a "learn-it-all" culture, emphasizing continuous learning and curiosity.
- Employee Well-being: Nadella prioritized employee well-being, recognizing its crucial role in productivity and overall organizational success.

- Participative Leadership: Nadella adopted a participative leadership style, encouraging open communication and collaboration.

- Collective Consciousness: As a transformative leader, Nadella focused on developing a shared organizational consciousness, making him acutely aware of the company's needs and potential.

- Empathy and Inclusion: Nadella worked to transform Microsoft's culture to be more empathetic and inclusive, reflecting his personal experiences and values.

Nadella and his leadership team executed the culture change through various initiatives:

- Communicating the vision clearly across the organization
- Leading by example, demonstrating the desired behaviors
- Aligning organizational systems and processes with the new cultural values
- Encouraging psychological safety to foster innovation and risk-taking

Under Nadella's leadership, Microsoft experienced a significant turnaround, regaining its position as a leader in the tech industry. The company saw improved financial performance, increased innovation, and enhanced employee satisfaction. This approach demonstrates how conscious leadership, focusing on culture, employee well-being, and continuous learning, can transform a large organization and drive sustainable success. This case study highlights Nadella's conscious approach to leadership, emphasizing cultural transformation, employee well-being, and fostering a growth mindset throughout the organization.[60]

2. Impact on Self-Discovery and Awareness

With AI, we have unprecedented access to vast amounts of personal data and the ability to derive deep insights from that data. This opens up intriguing possibilities for enhancing our self-awareness and understanding. AI can analyze patterns and trends in our behaviors, preferences, and routines, providing us with valuable feedback that can help us understand ourselves better. For example, AI-powered health and fitness apps and watches can track our physical activity, sleep patterns, and dietary habits, offering personalized recommendations for improvement based on how our body reacts to these outside stimuli. Similarly, mental health apps can monitor mood swings and stress levels, providing insights to help us manage our mental well-being more effectively.

In the workplace, AI can offer insights into our work habits and productivity, identifying areas where we excel and where we might need improvement. This can lead to more effective career development plans and personal growth strategies. For example, AI-driven performance analytics can help us understand our strengths and weaknesses, enabling us to focus on skill enhancement and career growth.

---

[60] *Career Insight: 5 Leadership Truths from Microsoft CEO Satya Nadella,* https://globalyouth.wharton.upenn.edu/articles/career-insight/career-insight-5-leadership-truths-from-microsoft-ceo-satya-nadella/, *From the Case Study on Satya Nadella* (docx) - Course Sidekick, https://www.coursesidekick.com/management/13595860, *Satya Nadella at Microsoft: Instilling a Growth Mindset,* https://publishing.london.edu/cases/satya-nadella-at-microsoft-instilling-a-growth-mindset/.

AI can also play a role in improving our interpersonal relationships. By analyzing communication patterns and social interactions, AI can offer suggestions on how to enhance our relationships with family, friends, and colleagues. This could involve understanding and improving our communication styles, recognizing emotional cues, and offering advice on conflict resolution.

As with most of what we're discussing throughout this book, it's important to approach this all with a sense of responsibility and ethics. While AI can provide profound insights, it's crucial to ensure that personal data is handled with the utmost care and privacy. Developing ethical guidelines and robust data protection measures is essential to ensure that the benefits of AI-driven insights do not come at the cost of personal privacy and security.

By leveraging AI to gain deeper insights into our personal data, we can significantly enhance our self-awareness and personal growth. This helps us understand ourselves better and empowers us to make informed decisions that can improve various aspects of our lives, from health and well-being to professional development and relationship building. The key is to use these insights responsibly, ensuring that our data is protected and our privacy is respected.

3. Impact on Decision-Making

Did you know that poor decision-making among leaders has been estimated to cost companies a minimum of 3% of profits? To put it in perspective, for a $5 billion dollar company, that's a $150 million loss—annually.[61] So, it's no surprise that more leaders and organizations are turning to AI to help close this data-insight gap by improving their decision-making. It's not that they're indecisive. It's simply that there is a lot of information, data, and decisions to be made. There's only so much one leader can do.

The human mind, while remarkable, has its limitations, of course. This is especially true when it comes to computing the vast array of possibilities and scenarios available in any given circumstance at any given time. This is where AI can impact LEAPers as a powerful ally. Because it is capable of processing and analyzing immense datasets quickly, it can help us consider a broader spectrum of possibilities and options and evaluate the scalability of each of them. This can be incredibly advantageous for LEAPers who never seem to have enough time in the day, providing a clearer picture of potential outcomes and guiding more informed decision-making.

According to an article about how AI can make us better leaders, there are numerous benefits—"Customer behavior, competitive analysis, and market trends are all areas where AI can provide intel, enabling leaders to be more proactive and strategic in their decision-making. As AI complements the human intuition and judgment that form the backbone of leadership, it can also deliver data-backed points that guide organizations toward success."[62]

---

[61] *How AI Can Help Leaders Make Better Decisions Under Pressure*, Harvard Business Review, https://hbr.org/2023/10/how-ai-can-help-leaders-make-better-decisions-under-pressure.
[62] *How AI Can Make Us Better Leaders*, Fast Company, https://www.fastcompany.com/90938516/how-ai-can-make-us-better-leaders.

This potential comes down to AI's ability to sift through substantial amounts of data quickly and accurately so that it can identify patterns, trends, and correlations that could easily elude the human mind's analysis. This capacity enables leaders not only to explore a wider range of options but also to foresee the implications of different strategies. For example, AI can analyze market trends, customer behaviors, and operational efficiencies in business to suggest optimal paths forward. In healthcare, it can predict disease outbreaks or suggest personalized treatment plans based on vast medical databases. In education, it can develop curriculums based on student needs.

This comes with a caveat, of course. The influx of information provided by AI can also lead to the risk of information overload and consequent burnout, which we will discuss in detail in Chapter 3. When leaders are presented with too much data, they may become overwhelmed and struggle to make decisive choices, finding themselves stuck in a state of analysis paralysis. To avoid this trap, it's crucial to implement strategies that streamline information processing and highlight the most relevant insights. It's also important to give enough time to digest it all.

To avoid this, LEAPers can benefit from setting up clear frameworks for decision-making that prioritize actionable intelligence over the sheer volume of data. This could involve using AI to filter and rank information based on its relevance and impact or priority to ensure that decision-makers focus on the most critical data points only. Additionally, incorporating intuitive AI interfaces that present data in a clear and digestible format can help prevent the cognitive overload that threatens effective leadership.

Another key aspect to informed decision-making is creating a culture of continuous learning and analytical skill development within leadership teams. By training leaders to better understand and interpret AI-generated insights, organizations can enhance their capacity to make informed decisions swiftly and confidently. This includes not only technical training but also developing skills such as critical thinking and emotional intelligence, which are essential for balancing data-driven insights with human judgment.

Ultimately, the strategic use of AI can empower leaders to make more precise and confident decisions. They can leverage a comprehensive view of the possibilities without being bogged down by excessive information. By embracing AI as a tool for enhancing human capability rather than replacing it, leaders can navigate the complexities of modern challenges more effectively while driving innovation and growth for their teams.

While the human mind cannot compute all the possibilities in existence, AI offers a means to broaden our perspective and consider various scenarios. According to an article in *Harvard Business Review*, "[m]ore and more businesses are turning to AI-powered technologies to help close the data-insight gap and improve their decision-making capabilities in time-critical, high-pressure situations. These technologies encompass a wide range of tools, including virtual assistants, virtual and augmented reality, process discovery, task mining, and an array of data analytics and business intelligence platforms."[63]

---

[63] *How AI Can Help Leaders Make Better Decisions Under Pressure*, Harvard Business Review, https://hbr.org/2023/10/how-ai-can-help-leaders-make-better-decisions-under-pressure.

This technological augmentation can greatly benefit leaders, provided they avoid the pitfalls of information overload and use AI insights wisely. By developing robust decision-making frameworks and enhancing analytical skills, leaders can harness the full potential of AI to drive informed, strategic decisions in an increasingly complex world. However, it doesn't take the place of independent thought processes. Ultimately, LEAPers cannot forget to make our own decisions. We can check with AI, but should not change our minds because of it.

4. Impact on Creativity

Artificial intelligence can be a powerful tool in the creative field (something that was previously thought untouchable). Yet, the juxtaposition remains—if we use AI for creative outlets, aren't we simultaneously losing our aptitude for creativity as humans? The answer, unfortunately, is, of course. The creative field requires intuition and emotion—it requires humans. We cannot lose this. But if we use it responsibly, here are several ways AI can be used to boost human creativity:

- **Idea Generation.** One of the most significant ways AI can help creatives is by helping them overcome creative blocks much sooner than they could on their own. AI can serve as a brainstorming partner by generating ideas, concepts, and possibilities that might not even occur to a human mind.

- **Collaborative Creation.** For those who like to collaborate in their creative efforts, AI can be an additional collaborator to produce new art forms, music, literature, and design. AI can suggest variations or continue a piece of work started by a human, offering new perspectives and ideas.

- **Enhancing Skills and Techniques.** Personalized tutorials, feedback, and practice exercises in fields such as drawing, music composition, writing, and more can assist an individual who wants to improve these skills.

- **Exploring New Forms of Art.** AI can enable the creation of art forms that might be impossible or extremely difficult to achieve manually, such as complex generative art, AI-driven installations, or interactive experiences.

- **Automation of Tedious Tasks.** By automating repetitive and time-consuming tasks that can even be present in creative fields, AI allows creators to focus more on their work's innovative and creative aspects.

- **Inspiration and Research.** Need a researcher? AI can analyze vast amounts of data to find patterns, trends, and insights that inspire new creative projects. Once a decision is made, it can also suggest materials, techniques, or themes to explore and enhance that project.

- **Personalized Content Creation.** AI can be used to create personalized experiences in storytelling, gaming, and interactive media, adapting the content in real-time based on reactions and choices.

- **Feedback and Revision.** AI-driven analytics can provide feedback on how a creation might be received by different audiences, suggest improvements, or help iterate on designs or stories based on user engagement data.

To keep tapping into and improving our own creativity alongside AI, it's essential to stay curious, keep learning, and remain open to new ideas and technologies. The key is using AI as a tool rather than allowing it to replace your own creativity. Engaging critically with AI outputs, understanding the underlying mechanisms, and actively choosing how and when to incorporate AI into the creative process can ensure that AI remains only a tool that amplifies human creativity rather than stifles it.

While opportunities remain abundant, the two areas to concentrate on for the most significant impact are upskilling and communication.

5. Impact on the Workforce

In the rapidly evolving landscape of technology and business, leaders must prioritize continuous learning and upskilling to stay ahead. While, as discussed above, AI may threaten many jobs, there are certain skills it cannot replicate. Take, for example, the healthcare setting. While AI can assist in making diagnoses based on symptoms, it cannot replace the physical presence of a nurse or doctor. The human touch and compassion provided by healthcare professionals will always be essential in human beings caring for other human beings. For nurses, the question of upskilling then may shift to how they can use AI to enhance their compassion in this setting even further. The rise of robotics may currently be limited to replacing redundant tasks under supervision, but the potential for expansion to make this field even better is vast. This is what it means to upskill in the age of artificial intelligence, but it is not limited to what AI says to do.

One effective way for leaders to upskill is by engaging in professional development programs, including executive education courses, certifications, and workshops that focus on emerging technologies, leadership strategies, and industry-specific trends. These programs provide leaders with up-to-date knowledge and practical skills that are essential for navigating contemporary challenges. Additionally, attending industry conferences and networking events can expose leaders to innovative ideas and innovative practices, fostering a culture of continuous improvement and adaptability within their organizations.

A crucial approach for leaders to upskill is to cultivate a learning mindset within themselves and within their teams. By promoting a culture that values curiosity, experimentation, and knowledge sharing, leaders can encourage employees to pursue professional development. Leaders can also leverage technology, such as online learning platforms and AI-driven training tools, to provide personalized and accessible learning opportunities for themselves and their teams. Mentorship and coaching, both giving and receiving, are also powerful ways to enhance leadership skills, as they provide real-time feedback and insights from diverse perspectives. By committing to lifelong learning and fostering an environment that supports growth, leaders can ensure they and their organizations remain competitive and resilient in an ever-changing world.

An important facet of developing the workforce in the age of AI is in talent acquisition. The question of whether human judgment and values should be prioritized over raw intelligence when hiring for a team. AI has the potential to make everyone more intelligent by providing access to vast amounts of knowledge and information, and by helping us to make better decisions. However, when it comes to hiring for a team, human judgment and values should still be prioritized over raw intelligence. This is because intelligence is not the only factor that matters, AI can't always replicate human judgment, and values are important. If you have 10 candidates who are all smarter than Elon Musk or Einstein, you would not necessarily select the smartest candidate. You would also consider other factors, such as their creativity, innovation skills, ability to work well in a team, communication and interpersonal skills, and values. By considering all of these factors, you can make a more informed decision about who to hire, and you can create a team that is more likely to be successful.

6. Impact on Communication

Much like the physicality in the healthcare example above, certain parts of interactions between a leader and team cannot be replaced or replicated. However, what we can do is use AI to improve those interactions. For example, we can program it to warn us when we are using condescending terms, terms that lack empathy and compassion, terms that induce fear, and terms that have a sexual undertone, among others, in our oral and written communications to others.

In addition to utilizing AI for communication enhancement, we can also leverage the power of storytelling and narratives in our interactions. AI has the power to tell strong narratives that we can use in our communication, but sincerity and integrity will always be the job of the LEAPer. The question then rests not on the fear that AI is taking something away from us but on how we can harness this power. This can be achieved by consistently practicing and honing these qualities through self-reflection and feedback from others. Remember, you want to harness your sincerity with the help of AI, not the other way around. Your word is your world. This is about quality. As Otto Scharmer noted, "The quality of our attention shapes the quality of our relationships."

7. Impact on Culture and Innovation

Organizations today face the dual challenge of keeping up with fast-paced technological advancements while nurturing a culture of creativity and innovation. To thrive in this dynamic landscape, LEAPers must be proactive, prioritizing flexibility, ongoing learning, and empowerment. Here are some relevant ways to help leaders navigate these challenges in line with our LEAP system:

— **Foster a Culture of Innovation**
- **Learning & Growth:**
  - o Embrace continuous learning for employees.
  - o Cultivate a learning culture that values curiosity and improvement.
- **Collaboration & Diversity:**
  - o Promote cross-disciplinary collaboration with diverse teams.
  - o Utilize collaboration tools to facilitate idea sharing.
- **Experimentation & Risk-Taking:**
  - o Foster a safe environment for experimentation with a "fail-fast" mentality.
  - o Support employees in exploring new ideas through initiatives like personal projects and seed funding.

— **Empower & Enable**
  • **Leadership & Management:**
    ○ Adapt leadership styles to empower teams with autonomy.
  • **Agile Practices:**
    ○ Embrace agile methodologies for flexibility and rapid adaptation.

— **Leverage Technology & Data**
  • **AI & Data:**
    ○ Leverage data and AI ethically for data-driven decisions.
    ○ Establish ethical guidelines for AI use.

— **Build Partnerships & Ecosystems**
  • **External Collaboration:**
    ○ Cultivate an innovative ecosystem with partnerships (academia, industry).

— **Focus on People & Vision**
  • **Employee Engagement:**
    ○ Communicate a clear vision for AI and innovation.
    ○ Celebrate successes to motivate and sustain momentum.
  • **Customer Focus:**

o Stay customer-focused by using customer insights and implementing user-centric design[64].

— **Drive Action**

- **Initiatives:**

    o Organize innovation challenges (hackathons, idea marathons).

This consolidated list provides a more concise and manageable overview of the key strategies for fostering a successful AI-driven innovation strategy.

Successfully navigating AI disruption demands a balance of embracing technological advancements while fostering human creativity. Organizations can remain resilient and innovative in the face of rapid market shifts by promoting a culture of learning, experimentation, and collaboration.

CASE STUDY 5: AI IN HEALTHCARE

As discussed earlier, the medical and nursing care landscape is undergoing a rapid transformation fueled by AI, robotics, and other disruptive technologies. There is perhaps no greater example of the enormous impact of AI on an industry that, at its foundation, is all about human beings caring for other human beings. Imagine a world where diagnostic tools possess superhuman accuracy, surgical procedures are performed with

---

[64] "The Importance of User-Centered Design in Product Development": Start Motion Media. (n.d.). The Importance of User-Centered Design in Product Development. Retrieved from https://www.startmotionmedia.com/the-importance-of-user-centered-design-in-product-development/

unprecedented precision, and patient care extends far beyond the hospital walls. This is the reality we are stepping into, with AI leading the charge.

In diagnostics and precision medicine, AI-powered image recognition algorithms analyze medical images like X-rays and MRIs with remarkable accuracy. These algorithms can detect anomalies that human eyes might miss, leading to faster diagnoses and earlier treatment interventions. Meanwhile, genomic sequencing allows us to decode an individual's genetic makeup, paving the way for far more personalized treatment plans. For instance, cancer therapies can now be tailored to target specific genetic mutations, maximizing their effectiveness.

Remote patient monitoring represents another LEAP forward because of the use of AI in healthcare. Wearable devices and sensors continuously track vital signs and health data in real-time, allowing physicians to monitor patients when they are not even physically present. This real-time data enables proactive interventions, potentially averting crises before they escalate.

Surgical and procedural advancements are equally groundbreaking. Robotic-assisted surgery, for example, allows for minimally invasive procedures with greater precision and reduced recovery times. Surgeons can perform intricate operations that would be challenging with human hands alone. Augmented reality (AR) is also making its way into the operating room, with surgeons donning headsets that overlay anatomical models onto patients, providing real-time visualization and guidance during delicate procedures. Additionally, 3D printing is revolutionizing healthcare by creating personalized prosthetics, implants, and even bio-printed artificial tissues.

In the area of care delivery and nursing practices outside the operating room, AI-powered chatbots and virtual assistants handle routine tasks, such as appointment scheduling and administrative queries, freeing up nurses to focus more on direct patient care and complex clinical situations. Telehealth and remote consultations are bringing healthcare closer to patients in remote areas or with limited mobility, improving access and reducing costs. Predictive analytics, also fueled by AI, can analyze patient data to identify individuals at high risk for specific diseases, allowing nurses to prioritize care and implement preventive measures.

But like other areas, there is a give and take—advantages and disadvantages, opportunities and risks. Challenges remain, despite these exciting advancements. Ethical considerations must be addressed, as AI algorithms can perpetuate biases and inequalities, which are already problematic in healthcare and create inequitable outcomes. Data privacy is another critical concern for patients who are at their most vulnerable moments in the healthcare setting. The integration of technology with human expertise must be seamless to maintain patient trust and deliver optimal care. Additionally, the healthcare work-force will need to adapt, with nurses and other professionals requiring training and support to navigate new technologies effectively.

The future of medicine and nursing care will be shaped by the leaders who embrace this disruptive landscape. By leveraging these advancements, they will improve patient outcomes, expand access to care, and revolutionize healthcare delivery. However, they must remain consciously aware of the potential risks and challenges by using AI as they LEAP into offering better, more robust, efficient, and all-encompassing healthcare.

SUCCESS BY DESIGN WITH AI

In the previous chapter, we evaluated the organization's readiness to adopt AI and developed a high-level action plan with your team to enhance AI readiness. This plan includes setting short-term and long-term goals, allocating resources, identifying training and development needs, and establishing governance and oversight mechanisms.

You will have also explored AI capabilities by researching AI applications that can benefit the business and pinpointing specific tools like CRM systems, predictive analytics, and chatbots that align with your objectives.

Now, it is time to drive success by integrating AI into execution and strategic planning using AI tools to analyze market trends, customer preferences, and operational efficiencies. Additionally, creating a road map that outlines how AI will be leveraged to achieve your strategic goals is crucial for success.

In my program, *LEAP Beyond Success*, I created the Success by Design framework for fulfilling strategies and goals as per the diagram below. In this book, I emphasize the importance of integrating AI into your operations to maximize its benefits. However, being cautious about completely replacing human teams with AI is crucial, as this could lead to the loss of essential human qualities in decision-making. AI can significantly improve your system by increasing productivity, relevance, efficiency, and accuracy at every stage.

To illustrate, consider using AI applications to assist you at each step of your process. By researching the market, you can find the most suitable app to help streamline your operations and enhance overall performance. Remember that AI should complement your team and enhance their capabilities rather than replace them entirely. By leveraging AI effectively, you can take your system to new heights of success.

SUCCESS BY DESIGN WITH AI:
A Framework for Fulfilling Strategies and Goals

DEVELOP YOUR
STRATEGY

STRATEGIC PRIORITIES
SELECTION

ITERATION   IDEATION

ALIGNMENT   ASSESSMENT

ADAPTATION

CELEBRATE SUCCESS   SET SMART AND
EACH STEP OF THE WAY   SMARTER GOALS

STRATEGIC PRIORITIES SELECTION

Your long-term strategy typically spans a three- to five-year period, serving as the foundation for your annual plan and the establishment of strategic goals and priorities. By having a clear vision of where you aim to be in the next several years, you can more easily determine the necessary steps to take within the next twelve months. Identifying which key thrusts and capabilities should take precedence and hold the highest priority is essential for success.

Choosing the strategic priorities for your organization is a critical decision that requires a thoughtful approach. Developing a process tailored to your organization's needs is key, whether that involves a committee of experts, market consultants, your mastermind group, or your board. These experts will assist you in selecting ideas that will propel your business or field forward. The selection of priorities should be informed by competitive data and an analysis of similar products or services offered by other companies.

AI can enhance the process of strategic priorities selection by analyzing vast amounts of data to identify trends, opportunities, and areas for improvement. AI algorithms can also provide predictive analytics to forecast potential outcomes of different strategic priorities, helping the committee of experts make more informed decisions.

It could be a committee of experts, market consultants, or your board—this committee of experts will select the idea or ideas that can advance your field or business based on regular brainstorming sessions. The selection of these goals is based on competitive data and comparative companies that offer the same products, services, and businesses.

Amazon uses AI algorithms to analyze customer data, market trends, and competitor information to identify strategic priorities for growth. This has helped Amazon to expand into new markets, launch successful products, and improve customer experience.

Another example is IBM, which uses AI to analyze market data and internal performance metrics to identify strategic priorities for its business units. This has helped IBM to focus on high-growth areas, such as cloud computing and artificial intelligence, while divesting from underperforming businesses.

Overall, AI can significantly enhance the process of strategic priorities selection by providing data-driven insights and predictive analytics to support decision-making. This can help businesses stay ahead of the competition and drive growth and innovation.

For instance, a retail company is looking to expand into new markets and increase their online presence. The committee of experts analyzes market trends and competitor data using AI to identify strategic priorities. They use AI to predict future market trends and opportunities, optimize resource allocation, and automate repetitive tasks to streamline processes. Based on this analysis, they decide to focus on launching a new e-commerce platform and targeting a younger demographic in their marketing campaigns.

Another example is of a technology company looking to stay ahead of the competition in the rapidly changing industry. The committee of experts uses AI to analyze market trends and competitor data to identify strategic priorities. They use AI to predict future market trends and opportunities, optimize resource allocation, and automate repetitive tasks to streamline processes. Based on this analysis, they decide to invest in developing new cutting-edge technology solutions and expanding their presence in emerging markets.

It is crucial to delve into the five dimensions of execution with AI. First, ideation plays a vital role in envisioning and foreseeing the future of your industry through opportunity discovery. Second, aligning your strategy with your core business is essential for successful implementation. Third, assessing AI programs and deep learning models that can be implemented across different departments is key. Fourth, adapting IT security, risk privacy, and governance to your organization is necessary. Last, adopting or integrating AI tools and programs across your departments is crucial for overall success.

1. Ideation

One way to enhance the ideation process using AI is to utilize natural language processing algorithms to analyze customer feedback, market trends, and competitor data to generate new ideas. AI can help identify patterns and insights that humans may overlook, leading to more innovative and effective ideas. A real business example of this is Coca-Cola, which uses AI-powered algorithms to analyze social media conversations, customer reviews, and sales data to generate new product ideas and marketing strategies. By leveraging AI, Coca-Cola can stay ahead of consumer trends and develop products that resonate with their target customer.

Another way to enhance the ideation process using AI is to use machine learning algorithms to predict the success of different ideas based on historical data. By analyzing past successes and failures, AI can help identify which ideas are most likely to be successful and should be further developed. A real business example of this is Netflix, which uses machine learning algorithms to analyze viewer data and predict which original content ideas are most likely to be successful. This allows Netflix to invest in content that is more likely to attract and retain subscribers, ultimately leading to greater business success.

2. Assessment

If your process yields a successful idea, it is important to capture the critical success factors for repeatability purposes. However, many ideas can fail. If they fail, your assessment of the causes of failure is imperative to determine if you should try the process again in a different way or let go of it.

AI can enhance this process by analyzing large amounts of data to identify patterns and trends that may indicate potential success or failure factors. By utilizing machine learning algorithms, AI can provide insights into the likelihood of success for a particular idea based on historical data. It can also help identify the root causes of failure by analyzing various factors, such as market trends, customer preferences, and competitor strategies. This can help in making informed decisions on whether to continue with the process or make necessary modifications for improved outcomes. Additionally, AI can provide real-time feedback and recommendations for continuous improvement of the idea-generation process.

3. Adaptation

Adaptation is a crucial step for innovation and the creation of novel ideas, products, and services. A successful idea may need periodic updates, requiring some form of adaptation of material, delivery, or timing. Failure does not always mean the idea was bad. It could simply mean the process needs to be changed. Or that, in order to execute, you need to adapt the idea and the process to your core competencies or develop new ones.

AI can assist in the adaptation process by analyzing data and feedback to identify areas that need improvement or change. For example, a company that uses AI to analyze customer feedback may discover that their product needs to be adapted to better meet customer needs. The company can improve customer satisfaction and increase sales by making these adaptations.

When Netflix first started as a DVD rental service, they quickly realized the shift toward streaming services. They adapted their business model to focus on streaming, which has led to their current success as a leading streaming platform. By adapting to the changing market trends, Netflix was able to stay relevant and continue to grow.

Apple continuously adapts their products to meet consumer demands and technological advancements. By regularly updating their products and services, Apple has maintained its position as a top player in the tech industry. This constant adaptation to changing trends and technologies has allowed Apple to stay ahead of the curve and remain competitive in the market.

4. Alignment

Aligning the project to the organization's mission and purpose is key. If the project is also aligned with your personal mission, a nice momentum for success is generated. AI can help enhance the process of alignment by analyzing vast amounts of data to identify trends and patterns that can help determine the best way to align a project with an organization's mission and purpose. For example, AI can analyze customer feedback, market trends, and competitor data to help determine the best strategy for aligning a new product launch with the company's overall mission.

AI can also help individuals align their personal mission with a project by analyzing their values, goals, and interests. For example, AI could analyze an individual's social media activity, work history, and personal preferences to help them determine how they can best contribute to a project in a way that aligns with their personal mission.

Overall, AI can provide valuable insights and recommendations to help ensure that a project is aligned with the organization's mission and the individual's personal mission, leading to greater success and fulfillment for all involved.

5. Iteration

Repeat, improve, repeat. Through iteration, you can continue the momentum of progress and innovation.

Companies create more success through variations, answer the market needs, and stay relevant.

AI can greatly enhance the iteration process by analyzing vast amounts of data to identify patterns and trends that can be used to make informed decisions on how to improve and iterate on a product or service.

Netflix uses AI algorithms to analyze user data and viewing habits to continuously iterate on its recommendation engine, providing users with personalized content recommendations that keep them engaged and coming back for more.

Amazon uses AI-powered analytics to track customer preferences and behaviors, allowing the company to iterate on its product offerings, pricing strategies, and marketing campaigns to better meet the needs of its customers and stay ahead of the competition.

TAKING ACTION

Executing from a new paradigm means redefining your leadership style, while staying in alignment with who you are as a leader and as a person. It means not losing sight of your own skills, unique abilities, and creativity but rather elevating them all with the tools that AI provides. It means reassuring your team that they need not be afraid of this change but should embrace it as the incredible opportunity it is. To do so, we should take the following actions:

1. **Foster a culture and team of agility and adaptability.** LEAPers understand that we cannot be rigid in our approach to leadership. We must continue to

adapt and evolve and encourage our teams to do the same. LEAPers need to be quick decision-makers and constantly seek out innovative solutions. They can only do this if they are agile enough to alter their approach as needed.

2. **Emphasize clear and transparent communication.** LEAPers use AI to help clarify our communication with our teams but do not use it to replace our communication, as we know our own voice and authenticity will be lost—and, along with it, the trust of our team.

3. **Embrace change and be open to new ideas.** LEAPers want to innovate and are open to learning new ideas from AI and any other collaborator.

4. **Elevate resiliency in the face of disruption.** LEAPers build resiliency by constantly putting ourselves out there, failing, and learning something new.

5. **Increase self-awareness.** LEAPers stay conscious and intentional in all that we do and say and every action we take.

6. **Don't start with AI.** LEAPers will always start with our research, our ideas, our creativity. They will ask—What do I sense is important to me and my voice? What is important to my creativity? What is ME? This is where we must start so that we don't lose our authentic creativity and voice. Then, we can use AI as a tool.

7. **Ask more questions of regulators and legislators.** LEAPers demand increased regulation by the EEOC and other regulatory bodies with oversight over AI.

8. **Rebuild core values.** LEAPers do this within ourselves and our team members.

9. **Remember accountability.** AI doesn't take the responsibility away from LEAPers to lead responsibly, ethically, and effectively.

10. **Consume less information.** LEAPers understand that we must spend more time digesting massive amounts of information to avoid burnout and information overload at all levels.

11. **Consistently work to ensure accuracy of information.** LEAPers will not use information without confirming that it is accurate first.

As in any aspect of life, an overabundance of power is anything but beneficial. Balance is key. This is truly where the imminent danger of AI resides. It can easily create superpowers and, consequently, increase inequalities that are already too disparate. As such, conscious awareness and ethics have never been more important than they are right now. By being mindful of what we are doing and what we are creating, we can choose to use AI for the collective good.

If left unchecked, AI has the potential to exert control over us. Rather than being fearful, as LEAPers, we must ask ourselves— How can we assert control over AI? How do we discern its intentions and leverage its capabilities to our advantage? These questions prompt reflection and demand enhanced awareness and consciousness.

With the understanding that no one has the answers to these questions, it's essential for us to contemplate these issues from various perspectives and remain vigilant. Perhaps a global forum dedicated to AI regulation will one day ensure consistency and accountability. However, even that has duality embedded into it, as excessive regulation risks stifling diversity and innovation, leading to a homogeneous world where uniqueness and creativity are victims. Striking the right balance will be crucial to harnessing the benefits of AI while preserving individuality and innovation.

CHAPTER 2 - EXERCISES AND TOOLS

Chapter 2: Exercise 1 - Enhance the strategic priorities process using AI

1. Analyze market trends and competitor data to identify strategic priorities: AI can be used to analyze vast amounts of market data, customer feedback, and competitor information to identify trends and opportunities in the market. This can help the committee of experts make informed decisions about which strategic priorities to focus on.

2. Predict future market trends and opportunities: AI can also be used to predict future market trends and opportunities based on historical data and patterns. This can help the committee of experts anticipate changes in the market and adjust their strategic priorities accordingly.

3. Optimize resource allocation and decision-making: AI can help optimize resource allocation by analyzing data on past performance, market trends, and competitor strategies to identify the most effective ways to achieve strategic priorities. This can help the committee of experts make data-driven decisions about where to allocate resources for maximum impact.

4. Automate repetitive tasks and streamline processes: AI can automate repetitive tasks and streamline processes, freeing up time for the committee of experts to focus on more strategic priorities. For example, AI-powered tools can automate data collection and analysis, freeing up time for the committee to focus on strategic decision-making.

Chapter 2: Exercise 2 - Ideation Using AI

Generate, select, and develop the sequence of ideas that move from the original concept to implementation. The chronology of the action plan should be discussed and evaluated. For this step, I recommend that your operational team be your best execution group.

- **Idea generation:** Use AI-powered tools such as idea-generation platforms or brainstorming apps to generate a wide range of ideas. Use AI to analyze data, trends, and patterns to develop innovative ideas.

- **Idea selection:** Use AI to assist in evaluating and selecting the most promising ideas based on criteria such as feasibility, impact, and alignment with organizational goals. AI algorithms can analyze data and feedback to prioritize ideas for further development.

- **Idea development:** Use AI to support the development of ideas by providing insights, recommendations, and predictions. For example, AI can help create prototypes, conduct simulations, or generate alternative solutions.

- **Chronology of the action plan:** Use AI to assist in creating a timeline and sequence of tasks for implementing the ideas. It can help set deadlines, assign resources, and monitor progress to ensure that the action plan stays on track.

- **Evaluation and feedback:** Use AI to analyze the performance and outcomes of implemented ideas to provide feedback for continuous improvement. It can help identify areas for optimization and suggest adjustments to the action plan.

- **Collaboration and communication:** AI can facilitate collaboration among team members by providing a platform for sharing ideas, discussing progress, and coordinating tasks. It can help streamline communication and ensure everyone is aligned with the action plan.

Here are some AI tools that you can use for the different steps, but remember that these tools are evolving every day:

- **Idea generation:** Use tools like OpenAI's GPT-3 or IBM Watson to generate ideas based on input data and prompts.

- **Idea selection:** Utilize AI algorithms like decision trees or neural networks to evaluate and rank ideas based on predefined criteria.

- **Idea development:** Use AI-powered tools like Google's DeepMind or Microsoft's Azure Machine Learning to assist in developing and refining ideas through predictive analytics and algorithmic suggestions.

- **Chronology of the action plan:** Use project management software with AI capabilities, such as Asana or Trello, to create a detailed timeline and task sequence for implementing ideas.

- **Evaluation and feedback:** Implement AI analytics tools like Tableau or IBM Watson Analytics to monitor the performance of implemented ideas and provide data-driven feedback for improvement.

- **Collaboration and communication:** Use AI-powered collaboration platforms like Slack or Microsoft Teams to facilitate real-time communication and collaboration among team members during the ideation and implementation process.

Chapter 2: Exercise 3 - Assessment Enhanced by AI

1. Choose a past idea that was either successful or failed in your organization.

2. Utilize AI tools such as IBM Watson or Google Cloud AI to analyze data related to the idea, including market trends, customer feedback, and competitor strategies.

3. Identify key success factors or causes of failure using the insights provided by the AI tools.

4. Reflect on how these factors influenced the outcome of the idea and whether they could have been predicted or mitigated.

5. Discuss with your team the implications of the analysis for future idea-generation processes and decision-making.

6. Implement any necessary adjustments or improvements based on the AI-generated recommendations to increase the likelihood of success for future ideas.

Chapter 2: Exercise 4 - Adaptation Enhanced by AI

- List different variations of an idea or product.

- Run simulations and experiments. AI can help identify which adaptations are most likely to be successful and provide insights into how to best implement them.

- Use predictive analytics. By analyzing data and trends, AI can help identify potential changes or adaptations that may be needed to improve the success of an idea or innovation.

One AI tool that can be used for this process is IBM Watson Analytics. This tool uses predictive analytics to help businesses analyze data and trends, identify potential changes or adaptations that may be needed, and make informed decisions about how to adapt their products or services. Watson Analytics can also help businesses test different variations of an idea or product using machine learning algorithms, allowing them to identify which adaptations are most likely to be successful. Overall, IBM Watson Analytics can help businesses adapt and innovate more effectively by providing data-driven insights and recommendations to guide decision-making.

Chapter 2: Exercise 5 - Alignment with organization's mission

Aligning a project with an organization's mission and purpose:

1. Create a project alignment matrix. This matrix should outline how each aspect of the project directly supports the organization's mission and goals.

2. Start by listing the organization's mission and goals.

3. Break down the project into specific tasks or deliverables.

4. For each task, identify how it contributes to the overall mission and goals of the organization.

5. Conduct a SWOT analysis (Strengths, Weaknesses, Opportunities, Threats) specifically focused on how the project aligns with the organization's mission and purpose. This analysis can help identify areas where the project may need to be adjusted or strengthened in order to better align with the organization's goals.

6. Finally, consider creating a project charter that clearly outlines the project's objectives, scope, and how it aligns with the organization's mission and purpose. This document can serve as a road map for keeping the project on track and ensuring alignment throughout the project life cycle.

This alignment with the organization's mission, purpose, and goals ensures that your actions are meaningful and impactful, driving you to continue leading from the new paradigm. Leaders can ensure that they are not only assessing data and information from AI applications, but also staying true to the mission of the organization. Ultimately, it is up to the leaders to make informed decisions based on both AI-driven insights and their own personal assessments in order to lead effectively and ethically.

ALIGNMENT MATRIX EXAMPLE

Organization's Mission and Goals:

- Mission: To improve access to education for underserved communities.

- Goal: Increase literacy rates in low-income neighborhoods by 20% within the next five years.

Project: Literacy Program for Underserved Communities

Task/Deliverable: Develop curriculum tailored to the needs of low-income students.

Alignment: This task directly supports the organization's mission by providing educational resources specifically designed for underserved communities, aligning with the goal to increase literacy rates in these areas.

Task/Deliverable: Recruit and train volunteer tutors from the local community.

Alignment: By involving community members in the project, you are fostering a sense of ownership and empowerment within the underserved neighborhoods, furthering the organization's mission to improve access to education for these communities.

Task/Deliverable: Implement a literacy program in local schools and community centers.

Alignment: This task directly contributes to the organization's goal of increasing literacy rates in low-income neighborhoods by providing structured educational opportunities in accessible locations for underserved populations.

Chapter 2: Exercise 6 - Iterative Improvement Challenge

Objective: To practice the concept of iteration by continuously improving a given task or process. You can use one or more AI tools for this exercise.

Instructions:

1. Choose a task or process that you want to improve. This could be a personal goal, a work-related project, or a creative endeavor.
2. Set a specific goal for the improvement. This could be to increase efficiency, enhance quality, or achieve a better outcome.

3. Break down the task or process into smaller steps or components.

4. Start by performing the task as you normally would.

5. Analyze the results and identify areas for improvement. Consider what changes could be made to enhance the outcome.

6. Implement one or more changes to the task or process based on your analysis.

7. Repeat the task with the implemented changes.

8. Analyze the results again and assess the impact of the changes made.

9. Repeat steps 6-8 as many times as necessary to achieve the desired improvement.

10. Reflect on the overall process and the progress made through iteration.

Benefits: This exercise will help you develop a mindset of continuous improvement and innovation. Practicing iteration can enhance your problem-solving skills, increase your adaptability, and drive positive change in your work and personal life.

Chapter 2: Exercise 7 - Building the 4 Wins Team Challenge

Objective: To demonstrate how focusing on the 4 wins (the leader wins, the organization wins, the people win, and the society wins) can lead to overall success and growth for everyone involved.

Instructions:

1. Divide your team into small teams of 4-6 people.

2. Each team will be given a scenario where they are tasked with coming up with a solution that benefits all 4 wins.

3. The scenarios can include challenges such as improving employee morale, increasing productivity, implementing sustainable practices, or giving back to the community.

4. Teams will have 30 minutes to brainstorm and come up with a plan that addresses all 4 wins.

5. After the brainstorming session, each team will present their plan to the rest of the group.

6. The group will then discuss and provide feedback on each plan, emphasizing how it aligns with the 4 wins.

7. Teams will have an additional 15 minutes to refine their plan based on the feedback received.

8. Finally, each team will present their final plan to the group, highlighting how it benefits the leader, the organization, the people, and the society.

9. The group will vote on the best plan based on its alignment with the 4 wins and overall creativity and feasibility.

10. Debrief as a group, discussing the importance of considering all 4 wins in decision-making and problem-solving processes.

This exercise will help participants understand the interconnectedness of the leader, organization, people, and society, and how focusing on all four can lead to sustainable success and a positive impact for everyone involved.

CHAPTER 3

ALIGN WELLNESS: MIND, BODY, AND AI

*"Leap into wellness with enthusiasm and commitment
and watch as your life transforms
before your eyes."*

- Andrew Weil

A s we move forward in the era of artificial intelligence (AI), it is essential that we prioritize human well-being and wellness in the development of these advanced technologies. The concept of aligning wellness involves integrating and balancing the health and well-being of the mind and body, along with the use of AI technology to support and enhance overall wellness practices. It emphasizes the importance of holistic approaches to wellness that encompass both physical and mental health, as well as the potential benefits of incorporating AI tools and resources into wellness routines. The fundamental question behind this chapter is: How can leaders stay ahead of the curve and adapt to the rapidly changing landscape of AI while preserving their wellness and wellbeing and preventing overwhelm?

It is our responsibility to take action and ensure that AI is aligned with the betterment of society. This can be achieved by placing human well-being at the forefront of outcomes and interactions, prioritizing human and societal wellness in the development of AI, safeguarding individual privacy within AI systems, developing human-centered AI frameworks, and upholding human control over AI behaviors. By considering these factors, stakeholders can work toward creating AI technologies that benefit humanity and protect individual rights and well-being. It is crucial that we take proactive steps to shape the future of AI in a way that enhances human life and promotes overall wellness.

LEAPers play a crucial role in influencing decision-making regarding the development of AI that prioritizes well-being and wellness by:

- Ensuring human well-being is at the forefront of outcomes and interactions
- Prioritizing human and societal well-being in the development of AI
- Safeguarding individual privacy within AI systems
- Developing human-centered AI frameworks
- Upholding human control over AI behaviors.

By considering these factors, stakeholders can work toward creating AI technologies that benefit humanity while also protecting individual rights and well-being.

The onslaught of information inundating us at rapid speeds, courtesy of AI, can be overwhelming for us all, especially for leaders, who are continuously concerned with more than just themselves. There have always been instances where too much of anything is not beneficial, and this is no exception. Information overload is a very real danger with AI and often results in heightened levels of stress and burnout. The constant access to all information—all the time—along with our own seemingly unlimited availability and accessibility with smartphones attached to our hands, instant meetings via Zoom, and technology everywhere we turn is leading us down a dark road—the end of which is the exact antithesis of all that we are trying to accomplish by enhancing our human intelligence.

Simply, how can we think, make decisions, trust our intuition, and act on higher levels if we are physically, mentally, and emotionally exhausted because we are constantly in a state of processing information?

The answer is—we can't.

LEAPers must shift our focus from merely acquiring information to *effectively* digesting and integrating it. And I emphasize the word effectively because we can think we are digesting information all day long, but just like when we digest food, proper, effective digestion takes time. There are no shortcuts to this, as much as we love our shortcuts to save more time to digest more information—and the dangerous cycle continues. Leaders generally do not take the time to properly absorb because no sooner do they turn around than there is more information to digest.

This is where the concept of aligning our body and mind for optimal wellness becomes crucial. In an age of artificial intelligence, where everything is moving faster than we ever thought possible, we need to step back, and yes, *we need to slow down.* Not all the time, of course, but we need to do it with more regularity than many are right now. Optimal wellness necessitates carving out time to disconnect and recharge amid the relentless flow of data so that we have adequate time and presence to process it all. Only then can we realize what information is relevant and what is not; what information is accurate and what is not; and what information we truly need and what we don't. Otherwise, our overwhelm becomes palpable, willing us to survive another day rather than thrive throughout our leadership ... and our life.

Life is all about balance. In the age of AI, LEAPers must balance productivity and well-being, and this is proving to be a critical challenge for many. With everything at our fingertips all the time, it has seemingly never been easier to get things done. And make no mistake; these things must get done. Key performance indicators must be met, goals must be accomplished, tasks must be completed, but at what cost? Stress and burnout have been increasing right along with our technological access. The direct link is very clear.

So, the conundrum exists—How is it that the thing that is supposed to be making our lives so much easier is actually increasing stress, anxiety, and other mental health issues?

Ironically, wellness, in this respect, is about both connection *and* disconnection. It's about connecting with ourselves (most importantly), connecting with nature, and connecting with others—those we lead and those in the world around us. At the same time, it is also about disconnecting from the thing that has the potential to quickly turn from helpful to harmful—our digital presence.

Make no mistake; by disconnecting to focus on wellness, I am not talking about spa treatments and expensive vacations. I am also not talking about never using our phones or computers again. I am talking about this ever-important connection—this link to what matters most to us—because we are so intensely focused on a small screen for most of our days. The wellness I am talking about is founded in the connections that can only be uncovered when we disconnect.

CONNECTION TO SELF, NATURE, AND OTHERS

Connecting with Ourselves and Balancing our Energy

LEAPers take the time to connect with ourselves because we know how much we benefit from enhanced self-awareness and emotional intelligence when we do so. "To lead consciously, we must cultivate self-awareness and compassion." Understanding our strengths, weaknesses, and emotions allows us to make more informed and authentic decisions, increasing trust with our teams. This self-awareness is key to enhancing our communication and empathy, enabling us to build stronger, more trusting relationships with our team members. Additionally, engaging in self-care and wellness practices helps leaders manage stress, maintain mental clarity, and prevent burnout, which is crucial for sustaining long-term leadership effectiveness.

Aligning our mind and body for optimal health is also about balancing our energy.

The East has a long history of knowledge and practice when it comes to energy. Practices like yoga, tai chi, and acupuncture are based on the belief that energy flows through the body, and balancing this energy is essential for health and well-being. In recent years, there has been a growing interest in Eastern practices and philosophies related to energy, leading to a more holistic approach to health and wellness in Western societies.

We will delve more into the energy concepts in Chapter 6, but for now, let's focus on the practices that will help us be better leaders of ourselves and others.

The following are a few tips on how to implement key strategies, such as:

- **Meditation.** A practice of focused attention or mindfulness that can help reduce stress, anxiety, and improve overall mental health. Practice mindfulness or guided meditation to tune into your inner thoughts and feelings. It doesn't have to be long, but it does need to be consistent.

- **Journaling.** Write down your thoughts, goals, and reflections to understand yourself better. This should be done daily, even if it is for a few minutes.

- **Yoga.** Engage in yoga to connect your mind and body through movement and breath. A practice that combines physical postures, breathing exercises, and meditation to promote physical and mental well-being.

- **Tai Chi.** An ancient Chinese martial art that involves slow, flowing movements to improve balance, flexibility, and mental clarity.

- **Acupuncture.** A traditional Chinese medicine practice that involves inserting thin needles into specific points on the body to promote healing and balance energy flow.

- **Reiki.** A Japanese energy healing technique that involves the laying on of hands to promote relaxation, stress reduction, and overall well-being.

- **Qigong.** A Chinese practice that combines movement, meditation, and breath work to cultivate and balance the body's energy.

- **Ayurveda.** An ancient Indian healing system that focuses on balancing the mind, body, and spirit through diet, lifestyle, and herbal remedies.

- **Hypnotherapy.** A therapeutic technique that uses guided relaxation, focused attention, and suggestion to help individuals make positive changes in their thoughts, feelings, and behaviors.

- **Breath work.** Various techniques that focus on conscious breathing patterns to reduce stress, increase energy, and promote relaxation. Yes, wellness can actually be as simple as the breath we take. Take time each day to focus on your breathing. This helps to center your thoughts and emotions.

- **Self-Care Routines.** Develop a routine that includes activities like reading, taking baths, or listening to music—whatever suits you and speaks to your soul.

- **Personal Hobbies.** Engage in activities you love, whether it's painting, playing an instrument, or cooking. Or learn a new hobby that you've always been interested in but never had the time to explore. This fosters a sense of joy and fulfillment.

- **Therapy or Counseling.** Talk with a professional to explore your inner world and work through any personal challenges.

- **Exercise.** Research shows that executives who exercise regularly are rated significantly higher on leadership effectiveness by their colleagues. Even short bursts of activity can be beneficial, with experts recommending multiple mini workouts throughout the day.[65] Exercise improves leadership effectiveness by:

  o Reducing stress and anxiety

  o Improving sleep quality

  o Boosting cognitive function and brain health

  o Increasing energy levels and stamina

  o Enhancing mood and optimism

- **Sleep.** Sleep quality significantly impacts a LEAPer's ability to manage stress in several ways:

  o Stress hormone regulation: Quality sleep helps decrease cortisol levels, the primary stress hormone. Lower cortisol allows leaders to respond more calmly to stressful situations.[66]

  o Improved cognitive function: Adequate sleep enhances concentration, decision-making, and

---

[65] *A Leader's Best Bet: Exercise,* Center for Creative Leadership, https://www.ccl.org/articles/leading-effectively-articles/spotlight-on-exercise-and-leadership/.

[66] *Fitness for Duty: Exercise Can Make You a Better Leader,* Forbes, https://www.forbes.com/sites/rodgerdeanduncan/2014/04/23/fitness-for-duty-exercise-can-make-you-a-better-leader/.

problem-solving abilities, which are crucial for effective leadership under pressure.[67]

o Emotional regulation: Well-rested leaders are better able to control their emotions and react appropriately to challenges, reducing anxiety and improving interpersonal interactions.[68]

o Enhanced resilience: Good sleep strengthens the immune system and improves overall physical health, making leaders more resilient to the physical effects of stress.[69]

o Better mood and outlook: Quality sleep boosts mood and optimism, helping leaders maintain a positive attitude when facing stressful situations.[70]

o Increased energy: Proper rest provides the energy needed to tackle demanding tasks and long workdays without becoming overwhelmed.[71]

o Improved memory and learning: Sleep facilitates memory consolidation and learning, enabling leaders to better retain and apply information in high-pressure environments.[72]

- **Eat Well.** Studies indicate that eating fruits and vegetables is associated with increased well-being, curiosity,

---

[67] *What Role Does Nutrition Play in Good Leadership?*, https://ilmovement.com/blog/what-role-does-nutrition-play-in-good-leadership/.
[68] *4 Components of Good Health and Effective Leadership*, https://www.ccl.org/articles/leading-effectively-articles/4-components-good-health-enhance-leadership/.
[69] *Ibid.*
[70] *Ibid.*
[71] *Ibid.*
[72] *What Role Does Nutrition Play in Good Leadership?*, https://ilmovement.com/blog/what-role-does-nutrition-play-in-good-leadership/.

and creativity. LEAPers are advised to focus on balanced meals with complex carbohydrates, lean proteins, and healthy fats to sustain energy throughout the day.[73] Nutrition plays a crucial role in enhancing leaders' wellness and effectiveness. Proper nutrition contributes to leadership performance by:

o Fueling cognitive function and decision-making abilities

o Maintaining consistent energy levels

o Improving mood and emotional stability

o Supporting overall health and immune function

Together, nutrition and exercise create a synergistic effect on health and leadership. They improve sleep quality, stress management, and overall resilience. By prioritizing these aspects, leaders can enhance their personal performance and set a positive example for their teams, ultimately contributing to better decision-making and organizational success.[74]

These are all great suggestions that can help with your wellness commitment, which, in turn, will help with your commitment to leadership. But if you want something specifically designed for you and your strengths, try asking AI!

CONNECTING WITH NATURE

Connecting with nature offers LEAPers a unique opportunity to recharge and gain perspective. Spending time outdoors

---

[73] *Is Nutrition Important in Leadership? Fueling Decision-Making,* https://www.linkedin.com/pulse/nutrition-important-leadership-fueling-performance-smart-njawaya-ap7lc.
[74] *Ibid.*

can reduce stress and improve mental well-being, leading to increased creativity and problem-solving abilities. Nature's tranquility is unmatched. It can provide a much-needed break from the fast-paced, high-pressure environment of leadership in the age of AI, allowing leaders to return to their roles with renewed energy and focus. Additionally, the practice of mindfulness in nature can help leaders cultivate patience and resilience. These are essential qualities for navigating the complexities and challenges of leading others, especially today. Here are a few great ways to connect with nature:

- **Hiking.** Explore trails and forests to immerse yourself in the natural environment. This is where all you can see, hear, and feel is nature with no distractions.

- **Gardening.** Some people find solace in getting their hands in the dirt and planting flowers, vegetables, or herbs to create a living connection with the earth.

- **Nature Walks.** Connecting to nature doesn't require a trip to the mountains or hours of gardening. Take leisurely walks in parks or natural reserves or even your own neighborhood to observe and appreciate the beauty around you.

- **Camping.** For some, spending a night or more in the wilderness is the best way to fully experience nature's rhythm.

- **Bird Watching.** Take time to observe and learn about the birds in your area.

- **Outdoor Sports.** Connecting with nature should be active, and there is no better activity than a sport you love. Engage in activities like kayaking, rock climbing, or cycling to enjoy nature actively.

- **Beach Time.** Remember, nature is not limited to mountains and rivers. Many people thrive by the sea. So, relax by the ocean, listen to the waves, and feel the sand between your toes.

- **Stargazing.** Connecting with nature can happen in the evening, too. Spend an evening under the stars, perhaps with a telescope, to connect with the vastness of the universe.

Similar to connecting with ourselves, if you want a way to connect with nature that is specifically designed for you and your strengths, try asking AI!

For those who want to get "more for their money" (or "time" in this sense), you can connect with yourself and with nature at the same time. This can be a deeply fulfilling and grounding experience. Here are some ways to do both:

- **Mindful Nature Walks.** Walk in nature, but be sure to focus on your senses while you do so, such as the sounds of birds or the feel of the breeze.

- **Nature Meditation.** Sit quietly in a natural setting, like a park or forest, and meditate there rather than your bedroom or living room.

- **Outdoor Journaling.** Bring your journal to a peaceful natural spot and write your reflections while being subtly influenced by your surroundings.

- **Forest Bathing.** Practice the Japanese art of "Shinrin-yoku" by immersing yourself in the forest atmosphere for relaxation and healing.

- **Yoga in Nature.** Practice yoga outdoors to combine the benefits of yoga with the calming effects of nature.

By integrating these practices into your life on a consistent basis, you can deepen your connections with yourself and the natural world and bring a sense of peace and well-being back into your leadership.

CONNECTING WITH OTHERS

As we have discussed throughout this book, in the age of AI especially, leaders must prioritize connecting with others by leveraging their emotional intelligence and human-centric skills that AI cannot replicate. Building strong relationships means better collaboration, enhanced innovation, and increased trust within teams, creating a supportive and dynamic work environment—one that not only gets things done but is also fulfilling and purpose-driven. By understanding and addressing their team members' unique needs and perspectives, leaders can inspire and motivate them, leading to increased productivity and job satisfaction. Additionally, these connections enable leaders to effectively manage change and navigate the ethical implications of AI, ensuring that technology is used responsibly and in ways that benefit both the organization and its people.

Connecting with others has truly never been more important than it is today. LEAPers must be able to motivate their teams to do what is most critical in achieving the organization's vision despite all the distractions. And motivation cannot exist without connection. There will never be a real commitment to a leader when their team does not feel that they are authentically cared about or invested in. This often comes down to the organizational culture we build.

So much of organizational culture comes down to human qualities. It is about how leaders create an environment where people want to come every day—a place where shared connections, values, and vision welcomes the team with open arms. But is there a way that AI can help leaders do this? Can AI help us go deeper in our cultural endeavors?

While this may sound counterintuitive, AI can help us connect to others and build stronger cultures. AI systems provide various insights about employees, including understanding their strengths and weaknesses and the areas of their work they are most passionate about. Armed with this information, we can connect more authentically. As noted in an article in *Fast Company*, "This could occur through behavioral science, in areas like versioning, simulating dialogues, and crafting relevant analogies. As leaders, we could use these insights to better connect with our team members on an individual level, constructing an environment where every employee feels valued and motivated."[75]

In today's dynamic organizational environment, fostering a culture of supported learning and aligning it with core values is essential for long-term success. Organizations need to develop a strong culture emphasizing continuous learning and adaptability, ensuring these principles are deeply embedded within the core values. This alignment is achieved through transparent communication and active involvement from leadership. Once LEAPers clearly articulate the organization's vision, they must

---

[75] *How AI Can Make Us Better Leaders*, https://www.fastcompany.com/90938516/how-ai-can-make-us-better-leaders.

demonstrate how the culture specifically aligns with it, along with the overall mission and objectives.

It's also crucial for LEAPers to make timely decisions and model the desired behaviors in the organization's culture. Delays in decision-making can hinder progress and breed uncertainty— two issues no one wants prevalent in culture. To ensure effective decision-making while using AI, LEAPers should prioritize fact-checking and identifying embedded biases in AI-driven processes. Transparency is key; consumers and employees increasingly demand clarity about how decisions are made and the data that informs them. When others consistently seek transparency, it pressures organizations to adopt more stringent regulations and ethical standards as they scale. Studies indicate that AI-driven processes offer superior scalability compared to traditional methods, enabling companies to expand their capabilities across industries. This scalability nurtures an environment of supported learning and leads to the development of more precise and sophisticated predictive models. By leveraging these models, LEAPers can unlock new opportunities and drive innovation, ensuring they remain competitive in this ever-evolving landscape.

In the face of AI disruption and the numerous distractions it creates, LEAPers must also focus on creating and maintaining a culture of creativity and innovation. This is a space where we promote cross-disciplinary collaboration and create a safe environment for experimentation, creativity, innovation, and yes, even failure, as we adapt our leadership style. This helps us leverage data and AI ethically, cultivate an innovative ecosystem, and remain customer focused.

To build the right organizational culture—one that will last and keep employees motivated and inspired requires the human touch. It requires connection. As with everything else, LEAPers can use AI to help them come up with ways to do so, but ultimately, it will come down to the connection among the team members and specifically, their connection to the leader. It further helps prompt a collective awakening. By emphasizing the importance of this connection, LEAPers are empowering others to discover their true selves. Consequently, they will be more willing to embark on their own journeys of self-discovery, awareness, and success through connections of their own.

Beyond the individual and even the team impact, connecting with others can also help LEAPers promote overarching social change. LEAPers can leverage their influence to address global challenges and create positive social impact. By leveraging AI to address pressing issues such as world hunger, climate change, organic agriculture, green construction, and waste efficiency, organizations can invest in resources effectively, adapt to changes across the business landscape, and welcome innovation. Leading effectively through periods of social change like this similarly requires clear communication, empathy, empowerment, flexibility, adaptability, and a focus on training and development. By following these strategies, leaders can navigate uncertainty with confidence and guide others in their community toward success.

CASE STUDY: THE COSTS OF INTERRUPTIONS

A very real and costly consequence of a lack of connection with ourselves and others (and a failure to disconnect from technology) is the increased rate of interruptions. In the age of AI, technological interruptions increase drastically when human connections are readily put on the back burner. Think about the notification alerts on our phones and from our email programs, those little dings that seemingly demand our attention immediately. Think of how many times we say, "Oh, let me just respond to this email (or text) quickly. It will only take a minute!" Think of how many times that minute turns into hours. Without awareness and a connection to ourselves, these interruptions can easily go unchecked, further negatively impacting our wellness.

Interruptions aren't necessarily all bad, though. It has even been reported that some interruptions can be beneficial. The downside is the stress that comes from switching topics so rapidly throughout the workday. Dr. Gloria Mark, a professor at the University of California, Irvine, extensively researched this very topic. Her findings on the effects of distraction on productivity were originally published over 20 years ago in 2004, but have been famously cited ever since. She found that the average worker is interrupted every 11 minutes and takes 23 minutes and 15 seconds to fully recover from the distraction.[76] But it's not only about what it does to the mental and emotional

---

[76] *The Cost of Interrupted Work: More Speed and Stress,* https://ics.uci.edu/~gmark/chi08-mark.pdf.

rollercoaster it puts us on. It's also about the very real costs it involves.

What does this mean for leaders? It means that wellness is beyond what some may think of as the "intangible benefits" of taking a step back to care for ourselves. It means that it impacts us where leaders feel it most—the bottom line. We are talking about the cost of employees who end up getting sick or having an accident because they haven't prioritized their wellness and are burned out and exhausted, as well as the costs of technological interruptions when we never, or rarely, disconnect from technology.

Consider a company that has 55 employees with an average salary of $50,000 annually. Suppose each of them is distracted every 11 minutes, and it takes them 23 minutes and 15 seconds to fully recover and be reimmersed in their work and productive again. In that case, that company will pay $1,065,900 per year for lost productivity due to those interruptions. And this is a conservative estimate that only considers the direct costs of distractions. This alone should want us to ensure that our cultures reflect that our teams are disconnecting at times and focusing on their wellness, as we do the same.

DEVELOPING HUMAN-CENTERED AI FRAMEWORKS

It is entirely possible to program AI to consider wellness and mind–body alignment. To ensure that AI programs prioritize wellness in their decision-making processes, it is important to establish ethical guidelines, implement regulatory frameworks, involve users in the development process, monitor and evaluate programs regularly, and encourage collaboration between stakeholders. These measures can help to promote the development of AI systems that prioritize human well-being and address the specific concerns of users.

By incorporating data on physical health, mental well-being, and emotional balance into the AI algorithms, it can provide personalized recommendations and support to help individuals improve their overall wellness and achieve mind–body alignment.

This could include suggestions for healthy eating, exercise routines, mindfulness practices, and stress management techniques tailored to the individual's specific needs and goals. Additionally, AI could also track progress over time and adjust recommendations accordingly to optimize results.

These AI-powered wellness tools offer a unique and personalized approach to achieving mind–body alignment and overall well-being. By combining cutting-edge technology with expert knowledge in fitness, mental health, and self-care, these AI assistants provide users with the tools and support they need to take control of their health and happiness.

> With personalized workout plans, mental health support, self-care reminders, sleep tracking, and mindfulness coaching all at their fingertips, users can truly transform their lives and achieve a state of harmony between mind and body.

Taking Action

Not only is it possible to achieve wellness in the age of AI, but it's also never been more important to do so. This must be a priority for LEAPers to avoid the burnout associated with increased access to data and information overload in themselves and their teams. While it seems counterintuitive to shut off our computers and put down our phones today, it is exactly what we need to do—disconnect to reconnect to ourselves, nature, and others.

So, how exactly can one achieve wellness in the age of AI? To do so, we should take the following actions:

1. **Set Boundaries.** LEAPers establish clear boundaries around when and how we engage with technology and information. We designate specific times for checking emails or scrolling through newsfeeds. And most importantly, we stick to these boundaries.

2. **Prioritize Tasks.** LEAPers identify the most critical tasks that require our immediate attention and focus on those only. We delegate to others or defer less urgent matters to avoid feeling overwhelmed.

3. **Delegate Effectively.** LEAPers trust team members with responsibilities to reduce personal workload.

4. **Stay Informed, Not Overwhelmed.** LEAPers curate information sources to stay updated without being inundated.

5. **Embrace Flexibility.** LEAPers use their adaptation and agility, which are crucial for navigating disruptions successfully.

6. **Practice Mindfulness.** LEAPers incorporate mindfulness techniques into our daily routine to cultivate a sense of calm and presence amid the chaos. We do regular meditation or deep breathing exercises to help alleviate stress and enhance mental clarity.

7. **Develop a Growth Mindset.** Embrace challenges as opportunities for growth, not setbacks. Effort and perseverance are crucial for success, and failure is a normal part of learning. Understand that facing challenges head-on can lead to personal development and achievement.

8. **Take Breaks.** LEAPers schedule regular breaks throughout our day to step away from screens and recharge. Even brief pauses for a few moments can significantly boost productivity and prevent burnout.

9. **Engage in Physical Activity.** LEAPers incorporate physical activity into our routine to alleviate stress and promote overall well-being. Whether it's a brisk walk, yoga session, or gym workout, we find activities that help us unwind and rejuvenate.

10. **Connect with Nature.** LEAPers spend time outdoors and reconnect with nature to recharge our batteries. Even a short walk in the park or sitting in a garden can have a revitalizing effect on our mental state.

11. **Disconnect Regularly.** LEAPers set aside time each day to disconnect completely from digital devices and immerse ourselves in offline activities. We engage in hobbies, spend quality time with loved ones, simply indulge in some leisurely reading. We do this because we understand the physical, mental, emotional, and financial repercussions if we don't.

12. **Get a Good Night's Sleep.** LEAPers make sure they get enough sleep to recharge their bodies and minds. By prioritizing sleep quality, leaders can significantly enhance their ability to manage stress effectively,

leading to better decision-making, improved team dynamics, and overall organizational success.

13. **Develop Human-Centered AI Frameworks.** LEAPers can program AI to consider wellness and mind-body alignment. By embracing the future of wellness with these innovative AI assistants, leaders can unlock their full potential for a healthier, happier life.

Are we, in essence, going "back to the future?" Don't we, in fact, need to get back to the basics of nature, non-digital existence, and experiential learning, where we are engaged as an active participant in leadership and in life? Renowned physician, advocate, educator, and podcast host, Dr. Michael Hyman, may have said it best—"Jumping into wellness is like taking a leap of faith toward a healthier and happier version of yourself." By uncovering resilience and reinvention through focusing on wellness and connection with ourselves and others, LEAPers can more easily adapt and find solutions that are equally adaptable for their team. They can more clearly focus on both the challenges and opportunities they face in this rapidly changing world as they lead into an unknown future.

CHAPTER 3 - EXERCISES

Chapter 3: Exercise 1 - The Transparency, Sincerity, and Integrity Reflection

Instructions:

Take a few deep breaths and get into an alpha state while listening to the alpha wave sounds. Use the Alpha Beat to reach the Alpha Level of Mind. Use this when you want to meditate without a guiding voice. (You can download these on the internet or purchase the online LEAP courses). When you get comfortable and relaxed, then:

1. Take some time to reflect on your recent professional and personal interactions with others. I recommend that you choose one difficult relationship at a time.

2. Consider how well you have embodied the principles of transparency, sincerity, and integrity in these interactions.

3. Ask yourself the following questions:

   – Have I been honest and open in my communication with others (or the difficult person you chose)?

   – Have I shown genuine care and concern for the well-being of those around me (or the difficult person you chose)?

   – Have I made decisions that align with my values and principles?

4. Write down your thoughts and observations in a journal or notebook.

5. Identify areas where you can improve in terms of transparency, sincerity, and integrity.

6. Develop a plan of action to enhance your leadership skills in these areas.

7. Share your reflections and action plan with a mentor, coach, or trusted colleague for feedback and accountability.

8. Commit to practicing transparency, sincerity, and integrity in all your interactions moving forward.

Chapter 3: Exercise 2 - "The Authenticity Mirror"

- Gather with your team with no interruption.
- Reflect on your values, beliefs, and strengths as a leader.
- Pair up in twos; the partner serves as "mirror."

The exercise begins with each participant taking turns sharing their personal values, beliefs, and strengths with their partner. The partner's role is to reflect back what they hear, highlighting key points and providing feedback on how these qualities align with the participant's leadership style.

After both participants have had a chance to share and reflect, they are asked to switch roles. The exercise continues with each participant taking on the role of the mirror, providing feedback and reflections on their partner's values, beliefs, and strengths as a leader.

This exercise helps participants gain a deeper understanding of their own authenticity as a leader, as well as provide valuable feedback from a trusted peer. By engaging in this reflective process, participants can identify areas where they may need to make adjustments to align more closely with their authentic selves, leading to more effective and genuine leadership.

Chapter 3: Exercise 3 - Prioritizing Tasks

Objective: To practice identifying and prioritizing critical tasks to increase productivity and reduce feelings of overwhelm.

Instructions:

1. Make a list of all the tasks you need to complete, including work tasks, personal tasks, errands, etc.

2. Review the list and identify the tasks that are most critical and require immediate attention. These are tasks that have impending deadlines, are high-priority, or are time-sensitive.

3. Prioritize these critical tasks by numbering them in order of importance, with 1 being the most urgent.

4. Next, identify tasks that can be delegated to others or deferred to a later time. These are tasks that are less urgent or can be handled by someone else without compromising quality.

5. Delegate or defer these tasks accordingly, freeing up your time and mental space to focus on the most critical tasks.

6. Set aside dedicated time to work on each of the prioritized tasks, focusing solely on one task at a time to avoid feeling overwhelmed.

7. Monitor your progress and adjust your priorities as needed, staying focused on the most critical tasks at hand.

8. Reflect on how prioritizing tasks has helped you stay organized, focused, and productive. Share your insights with a partner or group to discuss strategies for effective task prioritization.

Chapter 3: Exercise 4 - Trust Walk

Objective: To build trust and confidence in team members by delegating responsibilities effectively and encourage playfulness as well. If this exercise is performed outdoors, it will provide a nice break and a feeling of adventure.

Instructions:

1. Divide the team into pairs, with one person as the leader and the other as the follower.

2. Blindfold the leader and have them stand at one end of the room or outdoor space.

3. The follower must guide the blindfolded leader through the space, avoiding obstacles and reaching a designated endpoint.

4. The follower must give clear, concise instructions and demonstrate trust in the leader's ability to follow them.

5. After completing the exercise, switch roles and repeat with the other team member as the leader.

6. Discuss how trust played a role in the exercise as a team and how effective delegation can lead to successful outcomes.

7. Reflect on how this exercise can be applied to delegating responsibilities within the team to reduce personal workload and empower team members.

Chapter 3: Exercise 5 - How to Incorporate Mindfulness into Your Daily Routine

1. Practice deep breathing, meditation, or nature walks daily.

2. Reflect on your values and purpose. Take some time to reflect on what truly matters to you and what drives you as a leader. Write down your core values and purpose, and use them as a guide for making decisions and leading others.

3. Seek feedback from others. Ask for feedback from your team, colleagues, and mentors on your leadership style and effectiveness. Use this feedback to identify areas for improvement and growth.

4. Set clear goals and priorities. Identify your key goals and priorities as a leader and create a plan for how you will achieve them. Break down your goals into smaller, actionable steps, and track your progress regularly.

5. Practice active listening. As a leader, it's important to listen to others and truly understand their perspectives. Practice active listening by giving your full attention, asking clarifying questions, and summarizing what you've heard.

6. Develop your emotional intelligence. Emotional intelligence is a key trait of effective leaders. Work on developing your self-awareness, self-regulation, empathy,

and social skills to better manage your emotions and relationships with others. (You can go back to Leap Beyond Success, read or listen to it, and get the online courses that accompany the Leap sequel.)

7. Build a support network. Surround yourself with a strong support network of mentors, colleagues, and friends who can guide, advise, and encourage you as you navigate your leadership journey.

8. Take care of yourself. Remember to prioritize self-care and well-being as a leader. Make time for activities that recharge you, such as exercise, hobbies, or spending time with loved ones.

9. Continuously learn and grow. Stay curious and open to new ideas and experiences. Seek learning opportunities, such as workshops, courses, or conferences, to expand your knowledge and skills as a leader.

10. Practice gratitude. Cultivate a mindset of gratitude by regularly reflecting on and appreciating the positive aspects of your leadership role and your impact on others. Express gratitude to your team and those who support you.

Chapter 3: Exercise 6 - Growth Mindset

Take 10 minutes each day to sit in a quiet space and practice mindfulness. Close your eyes and focus on your breath, taking deep inhales and exhales. Pay attention to any thoughts or feelings that arise without attaching any judgment to them. Simply observe and let them pass.

After your mindfulness practice, journal about your experience. Reflect on any insights or observations you had during the practice. Consider how you can apply a conscious mindset to your daily life and challenges you may be facing. What changes can you make to cultivate a more positive and growth-oriented mindset?

Repeat this exercise daily for a week and notice any shifts in your mindset and overall well-being. Remember, cultivating a conscious mindset takes practice and patience, but the benefits are worth it in the long run.

Chapter 3: Exercise 7 - Transform Your Challenges Using a Positive Growth Mindset

Sit quietly and take a few deep breaths.

1. List your most recent challenge or challenges.
2. Could you embrace this challenge and reframe it as you include opportunities for growth and learning?
3. Create a new positive frame for each one of them.
4. Believe in your ability to improve and develop new skills using AI.
5. Positive thinking: Practice gratitude and focus on the good in your life. Challenge negative thoughts and replace them with positive affirmations.
6. Intentionality: Set clear goals and intentions for yourself.

7. Make conscious choices that align with your values and purpose.

8. Mindfulness: Practice being present in the moment and fully engaging in your experiences. Pay attention to your thoughts and feelings without judgment.

CHAPTER 4

PROGRAM HUMAN INTELLIGENCE

"I fear the day that technology will surpass our human interaction. The world will have a generation of idiots."

- Albert Einstein

Albert Einstein also said, "The measure of intelligence is the ability to change." This quote emphasizes the importance of adaptability in intelligence, highlighting the ability to adjust one's thinking and approach in response to new information and circumstances. It suggests that being able to change and evolve is a key aspect of intelligence. For Einstein, the key to human intelligence is imagination rather than simply possessing knowledge.

Therefore, in the rapidly changing landscape of AI, leaders must be prepared to address the threat that AI poses to human intelligence and help humanity leap beyond it. The future of leadership depends on it.

In the age of AI, relying solely on IQ as a measure of intelligence has become increasingly obsolete, as it risks rendering humanity comparatively inadequate against advanced technologies. Traditional metrics like IQ fail to capture the full breadth of human cognitive capabilities. Intelligence transcends mere problem-solving and analytical skills; it encompasses a profound understanding of complex systems and the ability to synthesize knowledge across various domains. We should redefine intelligence and seek a new metric, maybe an "Integrative Intelligence Quotient" (IIQ), which assesses an individual's ability to understand and apply fundamental principles that govern both the mind and the universe. This redefined perspective views intelligence as a multi-faceted construct that includes emotional, social, and philosophical dimensions, urging society to recognize the diverse intellectual strengths inherent in all individuals. By adopting this broader definition, we can appreciate the rich tapestry of human intelligence and ensure that we do not diminish our own potential in the face of technological advancements.

Over the past several years, we've heard a lot about emotional intelligence (or EI) overall and specifically its impact on leadership. Conversation after conversation, article after article, definitively establish that emotional intelligence is a key ingredient that sets outstanding leaders apart from the rest of the pack. Today, we're talking about artificial intelligence and its impact on leadership. And even though we're talking about a different type of "intelligence," we simply cannot talk about it without talking about its ripple effect on a leader's emotional intelligence. The question that truly needs to be addressed in this "P segment" of the LEAP process is—

At the delicate intersection of EI and AI, where do we factor in a leader's human intelligence?

Answering this question begins with a better understanding of EI. It requires an awareness that, as many are concerned with, AI can threaten EI in certain ways, but also, as many are unaware of, it also has the incredible power to enhance it. This comes down to our conscious awareness of it all and how we choose to use artificial intelligence. I don't use the word "choose" lightly. As we will see throughout this book, so much of artificial intelligence, emotional intelligence, human intelligence, and leadership comes down to the choices we make. Whether we make them consciously with an awareness of their implications or unconsciously by following others (and not really leading at all) depends on us.

Take, for example, CEO of Microsoft, Satya Nadella, only the third CEO in the company's history. Following the famous Bill Gates could be a daunting prospect for even the most confident leader, but not for Nadella. Over the past decade, he has made a name for himself with his transformative leadership style, which emphasizes empathy, continuous learning, and embracing change—or you could say he made a name for himself with his emotional intelligence. Through a strong growth mindset and his ability to adapt and inspire, he created great innovation for the company. And now, he is embracing change again with a strategic shift toward cloud computing and artificial intelligence. Through his conscious execution, he revitalized Microsoft's culture and steered the company to new levels of success. He didn't do this blindly. He understands the connection between EI and AI. Without a fundamental understanding of the interplay between AI and EI, we can neither understand nor appreciate how we can program our human intelligence to better serve those we are charged with leading.

THE IMPACT OF ARTIFICIAL INTELLIGENCE ON EMOTIONAL INTELLIGENCE

According to an article in Harvard Business School Online, "Emotional intelligence is the ability to understand and manage your emotions, as well as recognize and influence the emotions of those around you."[77] The notion that emotional intelligence, rather than technical skills or someone's IQ, is pivotal in conscious leadership is widely acknowledged. Psychologist Daniel Goleman noted the importance of emotional intelligence in leadership more than a decade ago: "The most effective leaders are all alike in one crucial way: They all have a high degree of what has come to be known as emotional intelligence. It's not that IQ and technical skills are irrelevant. They do matter, but…they are the entry-level requirements for executive positions."[78]

Research from the global consulting firm Korn Ferry also revealed a clear connection between emotional intelligence and leadership style effectiveness.[79] Korn Ferry's Emotional and Social Competency Inventory (ESCI), a 360-degree survey, measures and groups 12 emotional and social intelligence competencies that distinguish outstanding performance into the four competency groups—Self-awareness, Self-manage-

---

[77] *Emotional Intelligence in Leadership*, https://online.hbs.edu/blog/post/emotional-intelligence-in-leadership.
[78] *Ibid.*
[79] *Relationship Between Emotional Intelligence and Leadership*, https://www.kornferry.com/insights/featured-topics/leadership/relationship-between-emotional-intelligence-and-leadership.

ment, Social Awareness, and Relationship Management.[80] These are the primary competencies for emotional intelligence. And when we take a step back, the link is abundantly clear— we see that each of these competencies is crucial to effective management.

This link between high emotional intelligence and effective leadership has been demonstrated in numerous ways. Having these interpersonal skills gives leaders access to more influencing tactics—an essential piece to the leading of others. Without those skills, they have to rely solely on data, which rarely makes anyone want to follow leaders in the pursuit of their vision. It has also been shown that leaders who lack EI create or, at a minimum, attribute to toxic workplace cultures, low employee morale, high employee turnover, and communication challenges.

Yet, today, specifically with increased reliance on artificial intelligence, there appears to be an emotional intelligence deficit among leadership, despite these dire consequences. This gap is now widening, where more leaders tend to rely on AI and technology for innovative solutions and strategies rather than open dialogue and collaboration with others on their team. But, as with any aspect of business, leadership, or life, it's not all negative. AI has many positive impacts on EI, including enhanced decision-making and increased empathy. To understand them, it's important first to understand some fundamental distinctions.

Unlike humans, who can make choices to be self-aware and manage their feelings, AI consists of algorithms without emotions, so

---

[80] *Ibid.*

it can't truly be emotionally self-aware. Although AI can mimic emotions, it doesn't actually feel them. With regard to feeling emotions, there are three forms of empathy—cognitive (understanding someone's perspective), emotional (reading their feelings), and empathic concern (caring about them). AI excels at cognitive empathy due to its language analysis skills. AI tools and platforms can read emotional cues like facial expressions and tone of voice (oral or written). However, its ability to show empathic concern depends on its programming, which could be designed to support and nurture or, if misused, to harm. This is a key piece, as we will not know how it was programmed and, as such, will not know the basis for any particular response. If it was programmed to do harm, and we get negative responses over time to do so, it could impact our EI negatively.

Human qualities like "presence," which involve paying full attention to others, are difficult for AI to replicate authentically. And as we know with any leadership, trust, which is often founded in the authenticity that results from being present, is paramount. Without trust, there will be no one to lead. This brings us to a conundrum that exists today in AI usage among leaders—trust still appears to be lacking for major decisions and impacts, despite its overall increased use.

A MATTER OF TRUST

According to a study published in *Forbes* on attitudes toward AI, most don't think AI is quite ready to take over.[81] Consider the following responses:

---

[81] *Research Shows While Most Americans Are Aware of AI, Few Pretend to Know How It Works — and Three-Quarters Wouldn't Even Let It Pick Out What They Wear to Work*, https://krista.ai/ai-trust-survey-2023/.

- 67% don't want AI to make life-or-death decisions in war
- 64% don't want AI as a jury in a trial
- 57% don't want AI to fly airplanes

"When presented with scenarios that directly or indirectly affect them, Americans still trust humans over AI by a wide margin," a report by AI company Krista Software based on a survey of 1,000 American adults noted. "Americans aren't yet willing to allow AI to make decisions or work tasks where the outcome will potentially affect them."[82]

People also believe that humans will do a better job in a wide range of activities:

- investigating corruption (65%)
- choosing gifts (67%)
- deciding on a raise at work (69%)
- teaching a morality course (73%)
- administering medicine (73%)
- picking work outfits (75%)
- writing laws (76%)
- voting (79%)
- doing our jobs (86%)[83]

---

[82] *Ibid.*
[83] *Ibid.*

POSITIVE IMPACTS OF AI ON EMOTIONAL INTELLIGENCE IN LEADERS

1. Enhanced Empathy and Understanding

- Sentiment Analysis. AI tools analyze communication patterns, emails, and social media to gauge the emotional tone of employees. This analysis provides leaders with insights into their team's feelings and overall team morale, giving leaders a valuable tool for assessing the sentiment of the team and individual team member satisfaction. It's crucial to maintain relationships and connections. AI can help by detecting and correcting language that lacks empathy or induces fear, ensuring communication remains respectful and inclusive.

- Personalized Interactions. Understanding the emotions of the team, in turn, helps leaders respond appropriately based on the specific emotions they are displaying. In this way, AI helps leaders tailor their interactions based on individual preferences and emotional states, making communication more effective and empathetic. The result of this increased empathy and understanding and more appropriate responses is likely to increase the employee retention rate.

2. Improved Decision-Making

- Data-Driven Insights. AI provides leaders with more than an analysis of feelings, though. It also provides comprehensive data on employee engagement and satisfaction through certain data points.

By compiling data and outcomes, AI aids in decision-making and provides better matching and consulting services, helping us execute our purpose with greater precision and effectiveness. Having this information enables leaders to make more informed and emotionally intelligent decisions.

- Predictive Analytics. With an understanding of these data points and what they mean regarding their impact on emotions, AI can predict when trouble is brewing. By predicting potential conflicts or dissatisfaction, AI allows leaders to proactively address issues before they escalate. This encompasses a key component in employee satisfaction and overall nurtures a far healthier work environment.

3. **Continuous Learning and Development**
   - Feedback and Coaching. A large part of leading is developing others to lead alongside us one day. This requires continuous feedback that can be used for additional professional development and coaching. AI-driven platforms offer real-time feedback and customized coaching, helping leaders continuously improve their own emotional intelligence skills and those of the team.

   - Training Programs. Customized AI-based training programs enhance a leader's emotional intelligence by focusing on areas where they need improvement most. These platforms use advanced algorithms to analyze performance, strengths, and weaknesses and then recommend specific resources to help fill the gaps uncovered. An example of this type of training program is the popular one offered by social media giant LinkedIn. LinkedIn Learning is a platform based on AI-driven personalized course recommendations centered around a person's position, interests, and past learning behavior.

NEGATIVE IMPACTS OF AI ON EMOTIONAL INTELLIGENCE IN LEADERS

1. Overreliance on Technology

- Reduced Human Interaction. Dependence on AI to understand emotions has the potential to lead to a reduction in face-to-face interactions, which we are already seeing in many workplaces. Yet, these interactions are crucial for developing genuine empathy and emotional intelligence. The point is that while AI can be helpful for many reasons, as noted above, we cannot solely rely on it.

- Loss of Personal Touch. Leaders who rely too heavily on AI-generated insights and data potentially miss the nuances that can only come from direct, personal communication with their team members. We may be able to fundamentally understand their emotions but miss something important that we would have otherwise gotten from a facial expression or body language in a conversation with them.

2. Bias and Ethical Concerns

- Algorithmic Bias. AI systems can perpetuate existing biases present in the data they were trained on.

It all comes down to their programming, which is 100% done by humans—humans with their preconceived notions, biases, and inherent judgments. This can easily lead to skewed insights and unfair treatment of employees—the exact opposite of what any leader should want.

- Privacy Issues. Using AI to monitor emotions and behaviors is already raising significant privacy concerns among employees. They don't want every word, behavior, and conversation analyzed. They don't want a digital rendition of themselves for their employers to use as they deem fit. This can increase the mistrust already present with AI, as noted above, and increase mistrust with the leaders, while reducing morale.

3. Dehumanization of Leadership

- Impersonal Decision-Making. While we talked about the opportunity for more personalized responses in using AI appropriately, leaders also may make decisions based solely on AI data without considering the human aspect. This can have the opposite effect, leading to decisions that lack compassion and understanding.

- Emotional Disconnect. Reliance on AI has the power to create an emotional disconnect between leaders and their teams. Once again, nothing can or should replace genuine human interactions in building the strong, trust-based relationship required for employee productivity, satisfaction, and long-term retention.

So, while AI can significantly enhance a leader's emotional intelligence in many ways, including providing valuable insights and improving decision-making, it also poses inherent risks related to overreliance, bias, and the potential dehumanization of leadership. It all comes down to balance. Balancing the use of AI with genuine human interaction is essential for maintaining and developing emotional intelligence in leaders. And this is where developing our human intelligence becomes crucially important.

CASE STUDY: ENHANCING EMPLOYEE PERFORMANCE REVIEWS

Employee performance reviews have been a routine business practice for any business with employees (or at least they should be). In traditional performance reviews, leaders rely on their observations, feedback from managers and peers, and self-reports from employees. While emotional intelligence helps leaders empathize with employees and understand their perspectives in this process, it can be extremely time-consuming and very subjective, potentially missing critical insights throughout the course of events.

Today, more employers are starting to use AI-augmented performance reviews. By integrating AI tools into the performance review process, leaders are enhancing their EI skills while making the process more efficient and insightful. Implementing these AI tools helps employers analyze a wide range of data points that would otherwise have to be manually gathered and reviewed, such as productivity metrics, project completion rates, peer feedback, and even sentiment analysis from internal communication platforms. But the tools can do more than analyze data as discussed above; some can also provide emotional insights through a sentiment analysis of the employee's communications (emails, messages), indicating their emotional state over time.

Before the review, an AI tool can generate a comprehensive Insight Report, highlighting key performance metrics, trends, and emotional insights about the employee. It can also produce an Emotionally Intelligent Context Report for the leader to understand not just the performance but also the emotional context of the employee's work experience. During the review, the leader can use their emotional intelligence by engaging the employee with empathy and understanding, acknowledging the emotional states and challenges faced by them, all as indicated by the AI insights. This is invaluable to leaders.

The AI-provided data helps the leader offer objective, data-driven feedback, reducing biases and focusing on actionable insights that can help with personalized goal setting and the development of productivity and goal-centered plans going forward. AI helps identify areas for improvement and strengths, but it doesn't stop there. Rather, it is combined with the leader's understanding of the employee's emotional needs and aspirations, leading to more personalized and motivating goal setting. The leader uses their emotional intelligence to ensure the employee feels supported and understood, allowing for a more positive and motivating environment for their own growth and development.

After the review, AI can help with follow-up and continuous improvement with real-time feedback. AI tools are available to continuously monitor and provide real-time feedback on the employee's progress toward their goals. This allows for timely interventions and an opportunity to provide ongoing support. Leaders can maintain regular check-ins, using their emotional intelligence to provide emotional support and encouragement, while they leverage AI to track progress and make necessary adjustments to their approach.

As mentioned, incentivizing new initiatives among your team members and implementing original and novel ideas not created by AI will keep you aligned with your commitment to harness human intelligence. Rewarding the employees based on executing from the new paradigm of leadership and success will allow you to positively impact society as a LEAPer.

By combining AI with emotional intelligence, leaders can conduct performance reviews that are more comprehensive, personalized, and efficient than the traditional methods. The AI provides objective data and trends, while the leader's EI ensures the process remains empathetic and supportive. This combination, and their own human intelligence, results in better, faster outcomes, such as improved employee performance, higher engagement, a more positive work environment, and increased retention.

HUMAN INTELLIGENCE VS. ARTIFICIAL INTELLIGENCE

Human intelligence can be distinguished from artificial intelligence by its ability to experience and imagine and generate novel ideas and make decisions based on experience and gut-felt intuition. By prioritizing ethical considerations and incorporating moral reasoning into decision-making processes and using the skills and qualities that only humans can possess, we can ensure that AI is used responsibly and for the benefit of society. Human intelligence can be honed further by cultivating critical thinking skills and skepticism toward information and technology. We cannot accept everything at face value (we never should, regardless of AI). By questioning assumptions, challenging biases, and evaluating evidence carefully, LEAPers will avoid being misled by AI and make informed decisions based on the sound reasoning found in human intelligence.

Our human intelligence can also be strengthened through collaboration and teamwork—not only with other humans but also with AI itself. As discussed, the positive impacts of AI on emotional intelligence ring true here. By working together with AI in a complementary, rather than a competitive, manner, LEAPers will have the ability to combine our unique strengths based on our emotional intelligence with the efficiency and accuracy of AI to achieve better outcomes faster than ever before. This is the sweet spot. The place where LEAPers can truly advance their teams to the next level.

By focusing on developing unique human capabilities, such as creativity, emotional intelligence, continuous learning, collaboration, ethical decision-making, and critical thinking, LEAPers can gain leverage over AI, ensuring that it remains a tool that serves human interests and values rather than a threat to our very existence.

DEVELOPING HUMAN INTELLIGENCE

Human intelligence is a complex and multifaceted concept that encompasses various aspects of mindset, skills, and decision-making. The key to programming it must start with LEAPers thinking in exponential, multidimensional, superimposed, and quantum ways instead of linear and sequential thinking. I refer to quantum thinking as a way of thinking that is inspired by the principles of quantum physics. It involves embracing uncertainty, interconnectedness, and the idea that multiple possibilities can exist simultaneously. Quantum thinking encourages us to think non-linearly, to consider different perspectives, and to be open to new ideas and possibilities. It can be applied to problem solving, decision-making, and creativity in various aspects of life.

The human mind functions similarly to a computer program, continuously processing information to generate our thoughts, feelings, and behaviors. Our intelligence, rooted in our brain's biological functions, is influenced by our life experiences, education, and social interactions. On the other hand, artificial intelligence replicates human intelligence through machines, utilizing algorithms and computer programs for tasks like speech recognition, decision-making, and problem solving that traditionally required human cognition. Despite their similarities, there is a notable distinction between human and artificial intelligence. As we navigate the integration of AI in leadership roles, it is crucial to strike a balance between leveraging its capabilities for enhanced efficiency and impact, while also maintaining control over its influence.

To do so, LEAPers will proactively develop their human intelligence to ensure they have leverage over any new AI or technology that impacts our leadership and the world. To start, we must remember to continuously emphasize our emotional intelligence and creativity. LEAPers will also be increasingly focused on adaptability, lifelong learning, authenticity, and leading social change, now more than ever in the age of AI.

Remember, humans have the ability to think creatively, adapt to new situations, and understand and express emotions. This is a fundamental difference with AI, which excels at tasks requiring logical reasoning and data analysis. As such, by developing these creative skills and even passions further, LEAPers can leverage our unique capabilities to outperform AI (yes, we can outperform it when we know where our strengths lie) in innovation, problem solving, creative outlets, and empathy.

We can incorporate AI for self-discovery and awareness. With access to more personal data and insights through behavior-tracking apps and emotional intelligence tools, AI can assist in self-improvement. By leveraging these tools, we can better understand what attracts us and refine our passions. In this way, LEAPers will take this opportunity to lean into our passions in enhancing our human intelligence. AI can help us explore new interests or deepen existing ones like never before.

We can develop new skills and try out more activities than we ever could before. If your passion is education, AI can keep you updated on emerging trends, enabling you to educate others in more effective ways. As another example, one of my passions is creating processes, and another one is developing people. You might be wondering—*How can AI help me enhance my skills in these areas?* Well, AI offers tools for better self-assessment, providing insights into my strengths and weaknesses, and even helping me uncover new passions. As such, it can help me develop the right process for developing others based on my own strengths. Once we know what we are working toward, AI can support the implementation of our goals by tracking key performance indicators (KPIs) and monitoring progress with machine learning, allowing for faster adjustments and improvements.

Flexibility is key in programming our human intelligence as we continue to adapt to the ever-changing, ever-evolving landscape of AI disruption and technological advancements. Having a learning mindset and continuously developing emotional intelligence, creativity, and innovation skills will allow LEAPers to stay ahead of the curve in this fast-paced environment. We want to cultivate creativity from a place of playfulness and joy to tap into our full potential (and that of our team) and drive meaningful change in the world. We want to make decisions based on data that are also intuitive, empathic, and have a deep understanding of the situation at hand. Living with purpose and aligning our awareness in these ways to the direction of expanding happiness and fulfillment is essential for human intelligence development. This is all still very possible as long as we stay aware and conscious of the choices we are making—as long as we stay LEAPers.

AVOID OVERRELIANCE

AI's capacity to analyze vast data and make decisions raises concerns about potential overreliance, potentially diminishing critical thinking, original ideation, and innovative capacity. The transformative societal impacts of AI underscore the urgent need for ethical guidelines, safety measures, and in-depth research on AI safety. It is crucial to prioritize meticulous design, strategic planning, and safety protocols to mitigate the associated risks. By shaping AI systems to reflect human qualities like critical thinking, empathy, social-emotional impact, intuition, conscious awareness, and creativity, we can harness AI.

There is a concern that overreliance on AI for pattern recognition could impact human cognitive skills. AI excels at pattern recognition and data processing, but its decisions are based on the data it is trained on, which could be biased or incomplete. As AI systems become more sophisticated, there is a risk that people might develop emotional attachments to them, potentially overlooking the fact that they are merely machines performing pattern recognition.[84] This reliance could lead to fewer critical evaluations of AI outputs and diminish human pattern recognition skills. By practicing pattern recognition regularly, you will be better equipped to navigate complex situations and make informed choices.

It is crucial for us to cultivate aspects of our human intelligence that AI is unable to develop. By focusing on these areas, we can achieve breakthroughs that AI cannot, as it will free us from repetitive, tedious tasks. Some key areas where human intelligence surpasses AI include:

1. Emotional intelligence: AI lacks the ability to truly understand and empathize with human emotions, as it lacks feelings and consciousness.

2. Creativity: AI may excel at generating ideas and solutions, but it often falls short when it comes to thinking abstractly and creating truly original concepts like humans can. Our unique abilities, such as creative thinking, emotional understanding, and complex decision-making, set us apart from artificial intelligence.

3. Intuition: Humans can make decisions based on gut feelings, instincts, and subconscious cues, something AI cannot replicate.

---

[84] *AI: Pattern Recognition Instead of Human Values,* https://www.cmich.edu/news/details/ai-pattern-recognition-instead-of-human-values.

4. Morality and ethics: AI operates on algorithms and data, lacking the ability to make moral judgments or discern right from wrong.

5. Adaptability: Humans can quickly adapt to new situations, learn from experiences, and apply knowledge in different contexts, a skill AI struggles with without explicit programming.

6. Physical connections: Through the integration of robotics, AI, and sensory development, robots will become more adept at carrying out human tasks and understanding our interactions. However, they will not possess a capacity for emotional connections, love, and compassion.

7. Sensory and sentient feelings and experiences are something AI cannot develop. While AI can relay descriptions, it cannot truly feel these sensations.

8. The ability to sense the extrasensory field of energy and the quantum field is another area where human intelligence surpasses AI.

9. Humans can perceive systems thinking development as holistic, analytical, abstract, conceptual, and relationship oriented, which is something AI cannot do.

HARNESS OUR HUMAN INTELLIGENCE

In the age of AI, the question of how we can harness our human intelligence becomes increasingly important. It's not just about keeping up with technology but about integrating our human experience into everything we do. For instance, in retail, the focus should shift from simply fulfilling customer orders to creating memorable experiences through personalized recommendations, exceptional service, and seamless interactions.

To truly adapt, we must learn to unlearn outdated methods and embrace new ways of thinking, like pivoting our strategies based on AI-driven insights. Thinking non-linearly allows us to make better use of AI's ability to identify patterns, helping us to recognize trends and make informed decisions. Enhancing our memory and practicing discernment are also crucial, especially in an age where misinformation is rampant. Fact-checking has become a vital skill to ensure that we stay informed and accurate.

Building confidence, connecting with ourselves and others, and even tapping into higher powers, are essential in maintaining a grounded, authentic presence in a technology-driven world. Developing intuition helps us navigate uncertainty, and relearning decision-making can balance the data provided by AI with our values and goals.

As we improve our intuitive decision-making skills and embrace our uniqueness, we can fully harness our human intelligence. While we are biological beings, there's an energetic aspect to explore that can further expand our potential. The evolving role of consciousness and the brain's machine-like capabilities raise profound questions about the future of intelligence and the boundaries between humans and AI.

By activating our "superbrain" through lifelong learning, unlearning, and cognitive enhancement, we position ourselves to thrive in this rapidly changing world. Intelligence isn't just about being smart; it's about how we use our knowledge to influence and impact the world. As AI continues to alter our reality, developing our human intelligence will help us navigate these changes with wisdom, ensuring we remain connected to our core values and humanity.

Taking Action

Programming the human mind is a complex and multifaceted process. The human mind is influenced by a wide range of factors including genetics, environment, experiences, and culture. However, according to Randy Jirtle, "[e]pigenetics can trump genetics. If you're dealt a bad hand, it may be possible to reshuffle the deck." There are various strategies that can be used to help shape and influence our minds or program our own human intelligence. To do so, we should take the following actions:

1. **Build a positive mindset and self-confidence.** Identify and change negative thought patterns and behaviors. LEAPers understand the importance of improving mental health and well-being.

2. **Practice mindfulness and meditation.** These practices help LEAPers cultivate awareness, be more focused, and regulate their emotional output, leading to a more balanced and resilient mind.

3. **Create the experience in everything you do, and prioritize human connections.**

   Social interactions and relationships have a significant impact on programming our human intelligence. Individuals often adopt the beliefs and behaviors of those around them. As such, LEAPers surround themselves with positive people, leaders, and, of course, other LEAPers.

4. **Pivot and adapt to new situations.** Unlearn outdated or ineffective ways, and embrace the new ways. AI can process vast amounts of data and identify patterns that may not be immediately obvious to humans, but we can fully take advantage of our brain's neuroplasticity. This is the brain's ability to adapt and change in response to experiences and stimuli. LEAPers will harness this energy to reprogram the mind through intentional practice and repetition. Challenge the status quo and enhance your ability to adapt. Practice being open to new ideas and perspectives and learn to embrace change as a natural part of life. Additionally, seek out opportunities to step outside of your comfort zone and challenge yourself to try new things regularly.

5. **Improve your thinking, memory, and your language.** Think in a non-linear way. Many possibilities exist at the same time, so being able to process information rapidly is an asset. Fact-check to combat fake news and misinformation. Improve your language as a powerful tool for communication, creativity, and expression. Improve your memory. In the age of AI, having a strong memory can give us a competitive edge.

6. **Connect to a higher purpose.** It is important to note that programming human intelligence should always be done ethically and with our well-being in mind. It is also important to recognize the limitations of our ability to fully control or manipulate the human mind, as each person's mind is unique and complex. LEAPers

understand, though, that our mind has the power to free itself from the past and connect to a significant purpose.

7. **Take control of our new reality.** Our subconscious mind acts as our autopilot, constantly following our experiences, focus, and beliefs. It operates 24/7 to shape our behavior and align it with our emotionalized thoughts, hopes, and desires. The seeds we plant in our subconscious mind will manifest in our lives, as it controls 95% of our reality. By reprogramming our subconscious mind, as LEAPers, we increase the likelihood of achieving our desired outcomes. When we understand and harness the power of our subconscious mind, we can truly shape our reality and create infinite possibilities.

8. **Develop and nurture aspects of human intelligence that AI is unable to mimic.** Intuition, for instance, plays a crucial role in making effective and timely decisions. Ensure that your choices are in harmony with your purpose, vision, values, and objectives. Embrace the chance to venture into the quantum realm and access boundless possibilities.

9. **Stay curious and learn new skills in diverse areas.** By continuously seeking out opportunities to expand their knowledge and expertise in various fields, LEAPers will be better equipped to adapt to new challenges and opportunities that arise in an ever-changing world.

10. **Take care of your mind and body for optimal health.** Prioritize your mental and physical well-being. It's important to take a break from constant information

overload (yes, you can survive without your devices glued to your hands) and focus on caring for your mind and body. Refer to Chapter 3 of this book for further guidance on achieving wellness.

01	Build a positive mindset and self-confidence	
02	Practice mindfulness and meditation	
03	Create the experience in everything you do and prioritize human connections	
04	Pivot and adapt to new situations	
05	Improve your thinking, memory and your language	
06	Connect to a higher purpose	
07	Take control of our new reality	
08	Develop and nurture aspects of human intelligence that AI is unable to mimic	
09	Stay curious and learn new skills in diverse areas	
10	Take care of your mind and body for optimal wellness	

Diagram 6

It's important to note that the process of programming our human intelligence is ever evolving. There will not be a finish line. How could there be when new technology is being introduced on a daily basis? Programming our human intelligence means a commitment to continuous learning and adaptation. LEAPers will constantly learn new skills, acquire knowledge in diverse areas, and adapt to changing environments. We understand that flexibility is key here. The days of leaders digging their heels in the sand and not budging are over.

CHAPTER 4 - EXERCISES

The exercises in this chapter are designed for team building and practice in the age of AI to enhance human intelligence and programming skills. It is recommended to practice these exercises without the use of AI in order to fully develop these skills.

Chapter 4: Exercise 1 - Team Pattern Recognition Challenge (Team building and practice)

Objective: To enhance leaders' ability to recognize patterns and make informed decisions based on those patterns. This exercise aims to help you and your team recognize patterns and trends in specific areas of focus, such as employee performance, market trends, customer behavior, etc. By analyzing data points and key information in various scenarios, you will be able to identify patterns that can guide your decision-making process.

Instructions :

1. Choose a specific area of focus for the exercise (e.g., employee performance, market trends, customer behavior, etc.)
   - Select your group of leaders, managers, or staff
   - Select a good time that works for everyone without interruptions
2. Present to your group a series of scenarios or case studies related to the chosen area of focus. Each scenario should contain a set of data points or key information that leaders must analyze to identify patterns.

Pattern recognition in business can also be applied in the boardroom for crisis prevention. One example of this is when a board member observes a consistent decrease in quarterly sales despite successful marketing campaigns and product launches. This pattern may indicate underlying issues beyond marketing or product quality, such as ineffective pricing strategies or evolving customer preferences. Leaders should analyze customer satisfaction surveys, sales channel performance, and competitive analysis to pinpoint the root cause of the problem. By using this method, hidden patterns can be uncovered, and proactive decisions can be made to avert potential crises.

1. Ask participants, management, or board members to study each scenario carefully and identify any patterns or trends they notice. Encourage them to consider both quantitative and qualitative data, as well as any relevant contextual factors.

2. Once the managers and board members have identified potential patterns, facilitate a group discussion where they can share their observations and insights with one another. Encourage them to discuss the significance of the patterns they have identified and how they could potentially impact decision-making.

3. Challenge participants on the management and/or board to come up with potential strategies or actions based on the patterns they have recognized. Encourage them to think creatively and consider alternative approaches to address the challenges or opportunities presented by the patterns.

4. Reflect on the exercise as a group and discuss any key takeaways or insights gained from the process. Encourage leaders, managers, and staff to continue practicing pattern recognition in their day-to-day decision-making to further enhance their skills in this area.

By regularly practicing pattern recognition in a structured and intentional manner, leaders can develop a more nuanced understanding of complex situations and make more informed decisions based on data-driven insights.

Chapter 4: Exercise 2 - Adaptability Challenge (Team building and Practice)

This challenge exercise is for you to practice with your team. The challenge involves setting up a series of unexpected scenarios or obstacles that participants must adapt to and overcome quickly.

Participants can be divided into teams and given a limited amount of time to come up with creative solutions to each scenario. These scenarios could range from last-minute changes in project requirements to unexpected technology failures.

The key to this exercise is to encourage participants to think on their feet, collaborate with team members, and be open to trying new approaches. By facing these challenges head-on, participants can practice adapting to disruptions and develop the agility needed to navigate them successfully in real-world situations.

After completing the Adaptability Challenge, participants can reflect on what they learned about their flexibility and identify strategies for incorporating adaptability into their daily work routines. This exercise can help build a culture of flexibility within a team or organization, leading to more effective responses to disruptions and improved overall performance.

Chapter 4: Exercise 3 - Cultivate Your Empathy Beyond AI (from *Leap Beyond Success*, page 81):

This exercise, when practiced, will help cultivate abilities that AI cannot develop. It is important for us to continue developing our empathy and emotional intelligence to stay ahead in our personal growth and understanding of others.

Practice Exercise: Put Yourself in Their Shoes!

Step 1. Make a list of the people on your team, in your department, or in your network with whom you would like to connect.

Step 2. Every day for the next week, pick one person from your list and connect with them, either in person, via phone, or through a video platform.

Step 3. Practice active listening. Just listen with compassion. Be with the person and connect with them by trying to understand where they are coming from. Try not to give your opinion, but just practice listening.

Step 4. Imagine you are the person you are listening to. Imagine their biggest dream. Imagine their biggest fear and feel with them.

Step 5. Every day, write in your notes what shifted for you with that person as you stepped into their shoes.

Chapter 4: Exercise 4 - Authentic Leadership in the Age of AI (Team building and Practice)

Authentic leadership and innovative leadership are essential components of conscious leadership and the LEAP process. By integrating these elements into their leadership practices, participants can develop a deeper understanding of themselves and their impact on others, ultimately leading to more effective and inspiring leadership. Through reflection, discussion, and hands-on activities, participants will gain valuable insights and skills to become more conscious, authentic, and innovative leaders in today's rapidly changing world.

Objective: To practice redefining leadership style and leveraging AI to enhance skills and creativity while staying true to core values as leaders and individuals.

Instructions:
Divide participants into small groups and assign each group one of the topics listed below. Ask them to brainstorm action items for their assigned topic aimed at enhancing Authentic Leadership as follows:

1. Foster a culture of agility and adaptability by promoting rapid decision-making and creative problem-solving. For instance, consider implementing regular brainstorming sessions to inspire innovative solutions. Additionally, creating cross-functional teams can enhance collaboration and flexibility within the organization.

2. Emphasize the importance of clear and transparent communication, leveraging AI to enhance rather than

overshadow our genuine voice. For instance, utilizing AI tools to streamline routine communication tasks, allowing more space for genuine interactions. Additionally, implementing explicit communication protocols and guidelines for all team members to adhere to.

3. Embrace change and new ideas, remaining open to learning and collaboration. Some suggested action items could include implementing regular training sessions on emerging technologies and industry trends to encourage continuous learning among team members. Additionally, consider establishing a platform for sharing and discussing new ideas within the organization to foster innovation and collaboration.

4. Foster resilience in times of disruption by embracing failures and setbacks as learning opportunities. Consider implementing team sessions to encourage sharing and learning from failures, as well as organizing resilience workshops and training sessions to help employees bounce back from setbacks.

5. Enhance self-awareness and intentionality in our actions by incorporating mindfulness practices into daily routines. Additionally, setting personal and professional development goals can help to encourage intentional actions.

6. Prioritize our own creativity and research efforts before relying on AI as a tool. Encourage employees to brainstorm and independently research solutions before turning to AI. Regularly assess the information and cross-reference it to ensure accuracy.

7. Advocate for enhanced oversight and accountability in the deployment of AI technologies. This may include establishing a dedicated committee to oversee and uphold ethical standards in AI usage within the organization, as well as collaborating with external entities to push for regulatory measures governing AI.

8. Strengthening our commitment to core values within ourselves and our teams is essential. Developing a recognition program centered around our core values and integrating them into performance evaluations and feedback sessions are effective strategies that our teams can further develop.

9. Remember our responsibility to lead ethically and effectively in the age of AI. One way to address this is by incorporating ethical decision-making training into leadership development programs. Additionally, establishing an ethics committee to oversee AI implementation can help ensure ethical practices are upheld.

10. Prior to taking any action, it is essential to ensure the information is accurate. This can be achieved by implementing fact-checking protocols and utilizing tools to verify the information. Additionally, providing training to team members on critical thinking skills can enhance their ability to evaluate information effectively.

Once each group has finished their list of action items, prompt them to consider how to integrate their proposed action ideas within the framework of success by design outlined in Chapter

2 of this book. Encourage participants to contemplate how they can effectively implement these actions in their respective leadership roles going forward. In wrapping up the exercise, emphasize the significance of leading with authenticity and innovation in the era of artificial intelligence.

CHAPTER 5

QUANTUM LEAP

"We are on the verge of a revolution—a quantum leap—in our understanding of the universe."

Stephen Hawking

Quantum leaps are sudden and significant changes or transformations that can lead to major breakthroughs or accomplishments, whether personal or professional. They involve taking a giant leap into the unknown and emerging on the other side transformed.

In leadership, quantum leaps can be transformative, resulting in a new and improved version of oneself. Quantum LEAPers transcend conventional management practices by focusing on the interconnectedness of all elements and harnessing the transformative power of the L.E.A.P framework to create a thriving and productive work environment. By tapping into the collective energy of their team, quantum LEAPers ignite inspiration, foster synergy, and propel outcomes beyond individual efforts.

Characteristics of quantum LEAPers include their willingness to take risks, intuition, creativity, effective communication, and ability to tap into the infinite energy of the universe.

Leaders like Satya Nadella, CEO of Microsoft, have taken quantum leaps by investing in renewable energy and reducing carbon footprint. Nadella's decision not only benefits the environment but also the business by reducing costs and appealing to sustainability-conscious customers. His leadership showcases how businesses can make a positive impact on the world and how leaders can make a quantum leap.

In today's complex business world, quantum LEAPership is becoming essential, surpassing traditional leadership approaches. By applying the principles of L.E.A.P, leaders can navigate the complexities of the modern landscape and guide their teams to extraordinary success. Quantum LEAPership represents a paradigm shift in understanding leadership and its impact on organizations, emphasizing adaptability, collaboration, and the cultivation of a positive energy field for sustainable growth and innovation.

In conclusion, quantum LEAP-ership empowers leaders to create thriving workplaces by harnessing the power of human intelligence, observation, and interconnectedness. Quantum LEAP-ership emphasizes the interdependence of organizational elements, mirroring the complexity of the business environment and AI's impact. Embracing Quantum LEAP-ership principles helps individuals understand these dynamics and make informed decisions about AI's implications.

THE INTERSECTION OF AI AND HUMAN CONSCIOUSNESS

The intersection of AI and human consciousness is crucial. AI can assist in creative processes and decision-making, but humans should make the final judgment. AI enhances support systems in professions requiring physical presence and compassionate care, such as nursing, by identifying inappropriate language. However, human empathy and connection remain essential.

AI provides vast information, but it cannot replicate human intuition and experience. Clearly defining the roles of AI and humans allows us to leverage their strengths. AI handles data-driven tasks and provides insights, while humans focus on emotional intelligence, ethics, and creativity. This balance harnesses AI's potential while preserving human qualities.

In the realm of artificial intelligence, a profound gap separates human consciousness from machine intelligence. As we explore the intricate complexities of sensory and sentient feelings, we discover a realm that AI may not be able to breach. While AI can excel in relaying descriptions and processing data, it currently lacks the ability to truly experience these sensations that are inherent to human experience. AI cannot sense the systems and fields around them in the same way that humans do.

Simultaneously we must harness the power of AI as a tool for exploration. Like intrepid explorers of old, we can utilize AI to push the boundaries of human knowledge, venturing into uncharted territories of scientific discovery, artistic expression, and social innovation.

By empowering AI to handle mundane tasks and automate routine processes, we liberate human minds to focus on higher-level thinking, collaborative problem-solving, and the cultivation of deeper human connection. This symbiotic relationship between human ingenuity and artificial intelligence presents an unprecedented opportunity to push the frontiers of human intelligence and unlock a new era of unprecedented human potential.

Moreover, the idea of sensing systems and manifesting desires is grounded in energy concepts that are more prevalent in Eastern beliefs and medicine. While these concepts have not been widely incorporated into mainstream Western medicine, they are gradually gaining acceptance as evidenced by the significant amount of money spent on alternative and complementary medicine in the US each year. According to the NIH, the United States spends approximately $30.2 billion annually on complementary and alternative medicine (CAM).[85]

It is crucial to approach these ideas and practices with an open mind and critical thinking, as they may not always be supported by concrete scientific evidence yet. However, it is important to recognize that Western science is constantly evolving, and what may not be fully understood today may be better understood in the future more so with the help of AI.

In the business world, we often focus solely on what is visible and measurable, neglecting the invisible forces that shape

---

[85] *Americans Spent $30.2 Billion Out-Of-Pocket On Complementary Health Approaches,* https://www.nccih.nih.gov/news/press-releases/americans-spent-302-billion-outofpocket-on-complementary-health-approaches

our actions and behaviors. Yet, in the quantum field, all possibilities exist simultaneously. By aligning with this field, and by opening ourselves up to the invisible dimension of the field, we gain the ability to transcend conventional thinking and tap into our highest future potential.

In contrast to the West's traditional focus on physical and materialistic interpretations of energy, the East has a rich tradition of understanding and working with energy. Ancient civilizations like China and India have utilized concepts like qi and prana for centuries to comprehend and influence energy within the body and surrounding environment. As discussed in Chapter 3, practices such as yoga, tai chi, and acupuncture are rooted in the idea that energy flows throughout the body and that maintaining a harmonious balance is crucial for overall well-being. In recent times, there has been a surge of interest in Eastern energy practices and philosophies in the West, fostering a more holistic approach to health and wellness in Western societies.

The convergence of AI and human consciousness is a compelling and intricate phenomenon. As we delve deeper into the realm of AI, it is crucial to recognize that humans possess the capacity to develop abilities that far exceed those of AI. Are you ready to transcend beyond AI and cultivate aspects of human intelligence that have yet to be fully realized, such as sensory systems and energy fields, in order to surpass the capabilities of AI?

SENSING THE FIELD OF ENERGY

Consider the idea that our thoughts are connected to an invisible energy that permeates the infinite expanse of space, also known as the universe. How is it possible that our individual thoughts have the power to manipulate the universe on a microscopic level, shaping our physical reality? Well, thoughts stem from ideas and beliefs, which trigger emotions in our bodies—energy in motion. If emotions are a form of energy, then the energy we emit into the universe becomes intertwined with everything else, as the universe is a vast web of interconnected entities. By influencing one aspect, we can potentially impact another. Entanglement shows us that the boundaries between the observer and the observed are not as clear-cut as we once thought. When we align with this understanding, we can tap into the true power of creation.

For instance, to connect to the field of energy in energy healing, practitioners at the Barbara Brennan School of Energy Medicine focus on developing their ability to sense and work with subtle energies. This involves honing their intuition, deepening their awareness of their own energy field, and learning to perceive the energy fields of others.

One way they connect to the energy field is, as previously discussed in Chapter 3, through meditation and visualization. By quieting the mind and tuning into their own energy, practitioners can become more attuned to the subtle energies around them. They may visualize themselves surrounded by a luminous energy field or imagine themselves connecting to a universal energy source.

Another way they connect to the energy field is through hands-on healing techniques. By placing their hands on or near a client's body, practitioners can sense and manipulate the flow of energy in the client's energy field. Through gentle touch and intention, they can help to balance and harmonize the client's energy, promoting healing on a physical, emotional, and spiritual level.

Overall, connecting to the field of energy in energy healing involves cultivating a deep awareness of the interconnected nature of all things and learning to work with subtle energies in a way that promotes healing and transformation.

ATTRACTING AND MANIFESTING

This concept can be applied to the Law of Attraction, the philosophical premise that gained global recognition years ago with the book *The Secret*. The Law of Attraction says that like attracts like. So, we attract circumstances, people, and objects into our lives based on our own thoughts and emotions. By believing that what we desire already exists in our reality and visualizing it as if it is already ours, we can manifest it into existence. However, before reaching this state of manifestation, it is crucial for the mind to be calm and connected to a higher power beyond our conscious understanding. Essentially, we must first be connected to the field.

One prominent figure who has used the Law of Attraction in his own life is Tony Robbins. Robbins is a well-known motivational speaker, author, and life coach who has helped millions of people achieve their goals and reach their full potential. He often speaks about the power of positive thinking, visualization, and taking inspired action to manifest one's desires.

Robbins believes that by aligning your thoughts, emotions, and actions with your goals, you can attract the circumstances and opportunities needed to make them a reality. He emphasizes the importance of focusing on what you want, rather than what you don't want, and maintaining a positive mindset even in the face of challenges.

Robbins himself has used these principles to overcome obstacles in his own life and achieve success in various areas, from his career to his personal relationships. By practicing gratitude, setting clear intentions, and taking consistent action toward his goals, Robbins has been able to manifest abundance and fulfillment in his life.

Overall, Tony Robbins is a great example of how the Law of Attraction can be applied to achieve personal and professional success. By harnessing the power of positive thinking and visualization, individuals can attract the people, circumstances, and opportunities needed to create the life they desire.

The mind does not naturally distinguish between reality and imagination; it requires intentional effort. According to Neville Goddard, when we vividly imagine and repeatedly visualize a desired scene in our minds, such as a wedding or driving a luxury car, using all our senses and emotions, we can actually create a new reality.[86] However, the key is to make the imagined scene as realistic as possible to confuse the mind into believing it is already real and in existence. We cannot think about "wanting it" or "one day in the future having it." Rather, we must feel that we are already in that reality right now. By consistently imagining our desires, we can manifest them in our lives through inner work.

---

[86] *Awakened Imagination and the Search,*
https://www.awakenedimaginationandthesearch.org/tag/awakened-imagination-and-the-search-by-neville-goddard.

"Assume the feeling of your wish fulfilled and observe where your attention goes," Goddard continued.[87] Once we have done the necessary inner work and truly believe our desired reality is already ours, the final step is to let go and enjoy life, trusting that our wishes, our very manifestations, will come true. The how and the when parts are not to be of concern to us. That's for the universe to take care of once we put that energy out there. Then, it is simply about allowing the magic to unfold.

Goddard suggests entering a "state akin to sleep" or a drowsy state, where the mind is receptive and relaxed enough to imagine without interference.[88] Effective methods to reach a deepened state of relaxation to access the field include breath work, visualization, and listening to alpha waves music. Alpha waves were discovered by German neurologist Hans Berger in 1924 and later utilized by José Silva in his Silva Mind Control technique.[89] By using binaural beats, music, visualizations, and affirmations, Silva's techniques help individuals enter alpha states, where the brain is more alert, energetic, and open to connecting with the universal field of energy. Alpha states can be accessed during sleep, daydreaming, or through intentional practices like deep meditation or self-hypnosis. Regularly accessing an alpha state can enhance memory, creativity, and intuition, and even help manage stress and reduce anxiety.

---

[87] *The Power of Awareness*, https://www.thepowerofawareness.org/chapter-ten.

[88] *The Power of the Subconscious Mind*, https://trendculprit.com/power-of-the-subconscious-mind.pdf.

[89] *The Inventor of Electroencephalography (EEG): Hans Berger (1873–1941)*, https://www.researchgate.net/publication/339725586_The_inventor_of_electroencephalography_EEG_Hans_Berger_1873-1941.

Personally, I have been using Silva's techniques of getting into alpha states for more than two decades while meditating, visualizing, or doing self-hypnosis. Many times, your brain will still be in an alpha state when you first wake up in the morning and will reenter it as you are drifting into sleep at night. Learning to access an alpha state will help you with memory, creativity, and intuition and, if used on a regular basis—even for short periods—you will be able to cope with stress more easily, and your anxiety will decrease.

Deepening our understanding of emotion and feeling is central to *LEAP Beyond AI* because it reminds us that we do, in fact, have something that AI does not—we have emotional intelligence, we have feelings, and we have an innate sense of energy. This heightened sensitivity is exactly what distinguishes us from AI, which lacks the capacity for such sensory perception. This is one of the primary ways that will continue to separate us from AI going forward—and it is this very ability that will provide us with the competitive edge we need over AI in the future.

Research on consciousness transformation has shown that individuals who engage in practices such as mindfulness and meditation can experience profound shifts in their perception and behavior.

Some ways to Manifest and Attract:

1. Cultivating a positive mindset: Focus on positive thoughts and emotions to align yourself with the high vibrational energy of the quantum field. This will help attract positive outcomes and manifest your desires more effectively.

2. Setting clear intentions: Clearly define your goals and intentions and visualize them as if they have already been achieved. This will help send a powerful message to the quantum field and align your energy with your desired outcomes.

3. Taking inspired action: Take inspired action toward your goals and dreams, trusting that the universe will support you in manifesting them. Follow your intuition and take steps that feel aligned with your intentions.

4. Practicing gratitude: Express gratitude for the blessings and abundance in your life, as this will help raise your vibration and attract more positive energy from the quantum field.

5. Letting go of resistance: Release any doubts, fears, or limiting beliefs that may be blocking the manifestation of your desires. Trust in the process and believe in your ability to create your own reality.

By incorporating these practices into your daily life, you can manifest your intentions and desires with ease. Remember that you have the ability to co-create your reality and bring your dreams to fruition through the energy of the quantum field.

LEADERSHIP THROUGH THE LENS OF QUANTUM LEAP PRINCIPLES

As business leaders, some of our main goals are to foster growth, innovation, and productivity. Just like the natural order of things, we are constantly evolving as individuals, building upon the progress of previous eras to transform into something new. This concept is also evident in the fields of science, mathematics, philosophy, or theology, where remarkable advancements have been made by standing on the shoulders of giants. We stand on the shoulders of leaders before us and work toward one day being the shoulders for others to stand upon.

As LEAPers, we possess the power to shape our collective future, much like Canada geese flying in V formation, aligning together to reach their destination. Our consciousness begins to create subtle shifts in how we interact with people and systems around us. We start perceiving these systems from a perspective that includes ourselves. Our mindfulness deepens, making us more present to our experiences and more aware of the consequences of our actions. We shift our focus from our individualistic ego to the broader social fields encompassing our immediate family, communities, interest groups, and even larger systems, such as the economy, politics, environment, and the world. Consciously, we transition from a self-centered mindset to one that embraces the interconnectedness of all. In doing so, we move beyond the notion of being just one individual and embrace the idea of oneness with the whole.

So, how can we transcend self-centeredness and embrace our interconnectedness with the systems around us and the universe?

To access LEAPership or practice Leadership Through the Lens of Quantum Leap Principles, we must understand these principles:

1. Interconnectedness: This implies a fundamental interconnectedness between all matter and energy in the universe, including ourselves.[90]Leaders recognize that all individuals within an organization are deeply connected. They understand that their actions and

[90] *Quantum and Electromagnetic Fields in Our Universe and Brain*, https://www.ncbi.nlm.nih.gov/pmc/articles/PMC8146693/.

decisions impact not only themselves but also their team members, the organization, and the broader community. This interconnectedness fosters a sense of unity and shared purpose.

2. Consciousness and Leadership: Effective leaders harness the power of their consciousness to inspire and motivate others. They recognize that their thoughts, beliefs, and emotions can influence the collective mindset and culture of the organization. By cultivating a positive and growth-oriented mindset, leaders create a supportive environment where individuals can thrive. Some researchers propose that quantum processes in the brain may play a role in consciousness.[91]

3. Holistic Perspective: Leaders adopt a holistic view of their organization, recognizing that it is not simply a collection of individuals but an interconnected system. They consider the interplay between different departments, functions, and stakeholders to make informed decisions that benefit the entire organization. This aligns with holistic perspectives on existence and consciousness.[92]

4. Energy-Based Existence: Leaders understand that organizations are composed of individuals who are energetic beings. They foster a culture of well-being and energy management, recognizing that healthy and motivated individuals contribute to a thriving organization. This suggests that we are fundamentally

---

[91] *Ibid.*
[92] *Quantum Manifestation: Co-Create a Life You Love with the Power*, https://www.ashleymelillo.com/blog/quantum-manifestation-creating-life-you-love.

energetic beings connected to the quantum field that underlies all of existence.[93]

5. Non-Locality: Effective leaders recognize that they can influence and connect with individuals beyond physical proximity. They cultivate strong relationships, build trust, and create a sense of belonging that transcends geographic boundaries. This non-local property of quantum systems could potentially explain phenomena like intuition or synchronicities in human experience.[94]

6. Infinite Possibilities: Leaders embrace the concept of infinite possibilities. They believe in their team's potential and empower them to explore new ideas and innovate. By fostering a culture of curiosity and experimentation, they unlock the organization's full potential. This concept aligns with ideas about human potential and our ability to influence our reality through consciousness and intention.[95]

---

[93] *Ibid.*

[94] *Finding Connections: Where Quantum Physics and Spirituality Meet,* https://www.lancasterfarming.com/country-life/family/finding-connections-where-quantum-physics-and-spirituality-meet/article_6a35965f-0cf2-594b-82e5-8d43b6e04d17.html.

[95] *8 Steps to Connect with the Universe and Create the Life You Want,* https://www.adamhall.solutions/blog/2021/2/26/8-steps-to-connect-with-the-universe-and-create-the-life-you-want.

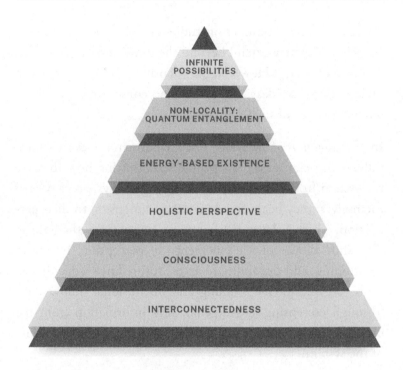

Diagram 7

In their book *The Systems View of Life*, F. Capra and P.L. Luisi emphasize the convergence between traditional philosophical perspectives and modern scientific insights, highlighting the interconnected nature of all things and events.[96]

Quantum Leap can be understood as a process of accessing a deeper level of consciousness that is aligned with our true selves and guided by our shared higher wisdom.

---

[96] *The Systems View of Life*, https://www.cambridge.org/core/books/systems-view-of-life/35186BA5B12161E469C4224B6076ADFE.

There have been a number of studies and theories that suggest consciousness may extend beyond the brain and be connected to a field of energy. However, the scientific community remains divided on these ideas, and there is no consensus on the existence or nature of such a connection.

In *The Essentials of Theory U*, Otto Scharmer argues that form follows consciousness.[97] As people start shifting how they see the system from being external to seeing the system as part of themselves, they begin to add another dimension to their perception, which Scharmer refers to as "presencing" the Source. This shift allows for the emergence of perception, intuition, envisioning, and the ability to access future knowledge. It also leads to evolutionary thinking and institutional innovations. Through co-sensing and downloading information from the outer fields, individuals can tap into a broader understanding of the system.

TAKING ACTION

By adhering to the four LEAP principles, we will naturally evolve into more mindful and cognizant leaders, enabling us to accomplish extraordinary short-term and long-term objectives. Moreover, through our interconnectedness with surrounding systems, we will experience a quantum leap in our leadership capabilities in the age of artificial intelligence. By doing so, our influence will go beyond personal goals and financial outcomes, resulting in a net impact that eclipses our individual aspirations. This is where we develop empathetic

---

[97] Scharmer, O. & Kaufer, K., *The Essentials of Theory U*, https://www.penguinrandomhouse.com/books/565259/the-essentials-of-theory-u-by-c-otto-scharmer-and-katrin-kaufer/.

compassion, cultivate intuition for effective LEAPership, and discern between our true selves and ego to lead authentically and with purpose. Ultimately, this alignment emphasizes the enduring need for connection between individuals and their environments, a need that AI cannot diminish.

Quantum Leap-ers develop essential skills such as flexibility, systems thinking, enhanced perception, intuition, and evolutionary thinking. By expanding their understanding of the systems around them and considering multiple perspectives, they can connect with their true selves and unlock their highest potential. Grounding their leadership in conscious awareness allows them to contribute to the greater good and align human intelligence with AI's capabilities. Embracing these principles helps leaders grasp the implications of AI on their organizations, employees, and society, fostering innovation and ethical decision-making in the midst of rapid technological advancements.

Follow these steps to make a quantum LEAP in your organization:

1. Inspire through purpose, aligning with the organization's mission and the quantum field.
2. Establish a new business model integrating AI. Integrate KPI metrics into AI programming for success.
3. Equip and empower people with necessary skills and tools.
4. Promote a learning culture and growth mindset and invest in continuous learning and development.
5. Lead authentically, with integrity, compassion, and focus on social impact.

6. Execute from the quadruple-win paradigm as you prioritize collective good and innovation.

7. Align your mind, body, and AI for optimal health.

8. Develop your human intelligence.

9. Embrace system thinking and Interconnectedness

This holistic approach, coupled with cultivating adaptive thinking skills like flexibility and considering multiple perspectives, will empower individuals and organizations to achieve quantum leaps in success and beyond, effectively navigating the challenges posed by AI.

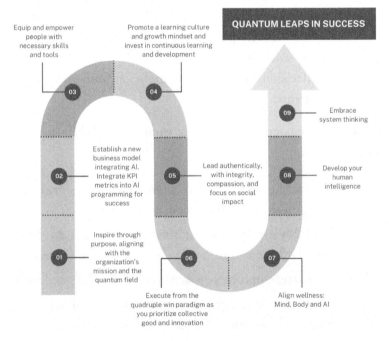

Diagram 8

CHAPTER 6

LEAP TO THE CONCLUSION ... FOR NOW

"In a world where experts caution against surrendering too much power to artificial intelligence, it is timely that this theory delivers a source of far greater empowerment: advanced human intelligence gained through the development of consciousness."

- Dr. Tony Nader

B y reaching this point in the book, it's clear you are already a conscious leader or LEAPer! You possess a heightened level of self-awareness and consciousness around your decisions and actions and want to elevate them even further in the age of artificial intelligence. The discussions, exercises, and examples we've explored throughout this book, as well as case studies and Take Action tips, will help you deepen your leadership even further.

Conscious leaders like you have undergone, or are undergoing, a journey of deep introspection and transformation. We've recognized and overcome the hidden fears that hold us back from our full potential, developing a keen awareness of the thoughts, emotions, and behaviors that allow us to make conscious choices and lead with intention. This is exactly what will be required of you as you navigate the AI waters of the future.

Engaging in these conversations enables us to collectively shape a future where AI enhances human capabilities and serves as a tool for societal progress rather than becoming a threat. By fostering a collaborative approach to AI governance, we can strive to create a balanced and equitable technological landscape that benefits all of humanity. And we will.

In my opinion, leaders need to recognize that disruption is not something to fear but rather an opportunity for growth and innovation. Disruption sparks new ideas and breakthroughs, and leaders embracing this mindset are likelier to succeed. They must be willing to challenge the status quo and push boundaries to achieve significant progress. Embracing disruption allows leaders to capitalize on emerging trends and technologies, fostering a culture of continuous improvement and adaptability.

The middle-of-the-road view of our future co-existence with AI is exactly what we are focusing on in these pages. We can't ignore the risks, nor should we, but we also can't operate in fear of what this all means. We need to get away from the doomsday scenarios as much as we need to get away from the cure-all scenarios and focus on the middle ground—the one that keeps us in control. As LEAPers, we will continue to talk about increased regulation and safeguards to minimize risks and potential downfalls. We will continue to tap into our human intelligence and use it more often than ever before, and we will continue to lead responsibly into the future.

In this era of AI disruption, the future of transformation is bright and exciting. Jim Hemerling's five imperatives for transforming organizations are paving the way for a new era of 'Always-On' innovation. By putting people first, organizations can inspire through purpose, go all in on new business models, build capabilities for the future, instill a learning culture, and lead inclusively. This positive and futuristic approach to transformation is revolutionizing the way businesses operate, ensuring they are prepared to thrive in the ever-evolving landscape of technology and disruption. The era of AI disruption is not a threat but an opportunity for organizations to embrace change and drive toward a brighter and more successful future.

THE EVOLUTION OF AI IN LEADERSHIP

Reflecting on the evolution of AI technology and its rapid advancements in recent years, it's easy to see its transformative power across various industries and functions.

The rapid advancement of artificial intelligence specifically artificial general intelligence (AGI) and potentially artificial super intelligence (ASI) is on the horizon. AGI has the potential to surpass human intelligence in various fields, while ASI could revolutionize the way we think and innovate. The implications of this technological progress are vast, with potential to disrupt and transform every aspect of society, including the job market and power dynamics.

The integration of AI with robotics will lead to more capable and adaptable robots that can operate in dynamic environments, enhancing applications in logistics, manufacturing, and service industries. The combination of robotics, AI, and sensory development may blur the lines of physicality, yet the importance of physical and emotional connections will continue to be relevant.

Genetic engineering technologies, such as gene therapy, gene manipulation, and gene selection, have the ability to alter the genetic makeup of living organisms. These advancements offer potential benefits in areas such as disease treatment, agriculture improvement, and trait selection. However, there are valid concerns regarding the misuse and unintended repercussions if not utilized responsibly. Ethical dilemmas are also a significant issue in the realm of genetic engineering, especially in human gene editing. The possibility of creating designer babies or enhancing traits beyond ethical boundaries raises ethical questions. Additionally, the impact of genetic engineering on biodiversity and the environment is a cause for concern. Introducing genetically modified organisms into ecosystems may have unforeseen effects on other species or disrupt natural ecosystems.

In addition, there is the potential for some humans to choose to merge with artificial intelligence in order to enhance their own cognitive abilities and become super intelligent beings. This concept, known as transhumanism, brings up ethical and philosophical questions about the implications of blurring the line between human and machine. By integrating AI technology into their own bodies and minds, individuals may be able to surpass the limitations of human intelligence and unlock new levels of creativity, problem solving, and understanding.

However, this merging of human and machine could be a source of concern about loss of individuality, privacy, and control over one's own thoughts and actions. Ultimately, the decision to merge with AI is a complex and deeply personal choice that each individual must carefully consider.

AI potential to revolutionize leadership practices is immense. But let's take it a step further. Revolutions like these offer unprecedented opportunities. By harnessing AI-powered tools and systems, leaders can access real-time insights, streamline processes, and foster a culture of continuous improvement.

The advantages of using AI in leadership are diverse and immense. AI can enhance decision-making, boost productivity, and spur innovation, providing leaders with the tools to navigate complex challenges with greater agility. However, these advancements also bring significant challenges, such as job displacement and the ethical considerations that accompany AI integration. The potential disadvantages simply cannot be ignored. If not carefully managed, AI could eventually control us, perpetuating biases, infringing on privacy, and widening socioeconomic disparities. Leaders must take proactive steps to control AI first, ensuring it serves humanity rather than undermining it.

It has been said that the next stage of generative AI will be even "more transformative," with technology moving from thought to action.[98] And it's already being embraced by leaders. Now

---

[98] *AI Agents Are the Next Frontier and Will Change Our Working Lives Forever,* https://www.zdnet.com/article/ai-agents-are-the-next-frontier-and-will-change -our-working-lives-forever/.

that AI can take on more diverse roles, "a virtual assistant, for example, could plan and book a complex personalized travel itinerary, handling logistics across multiple travel platforms," a McKinsey report said. "Using everyday language, an engineer could describe a new software feature to a programmer agent, which would then code, test, iterate, and deploy the tool it helped create."[99]

Further, a recent study of 1,100 tech executives by Capgemini showed the following results:

- 82% indicated they intend to integrate AI-based agents across their organizations within the next three years (up from 10% with functioning agents at the current time);

- 70% of respondents would trust an AI agent to analyze and synthesize data;

- 50% would trust an AI agent to send a professional email on their behalf;

- 75% said they intend to deploy AI agents to tackle tasks such as generating and iteratively improving code;

- 70% said they would use it to generate and edit draft reports, while 68% said they would use it to generate and draft website content and email generation, coding, and data analysis.[100]

To harness the full potential of AI, leaders must cultivate a mindset of continuous learning and adaptability. Embrace

---

[99] *Ibid.*
[100] *Generative AI in Organizations,* https://www.capgemini.com/insights/research-library/generative-ai-in-organizations-2024/.

the unknown, challenge the status quo, and push the boundaries of what is possible. By fostering a culture of curiosity and resilience, leaders can navigate the uncertainties of AI, turning potential threats into opportunities for growth and transformation.

The implications of AI for leadership dynamics within organizations are profound. While AI can augment human capabilities and drive more informed decision-making, it also necessitates a reevaluation of traditional leadership roles and responsibilities. Leaders must navigate the complexities of AI implementation, ensuring that technology complements rather than replaces human intuition and emotional intelligence. This balance is crucial in maintaining a humane and empathetic approach to leadership.

LEAPERSHIP: BEYOND MANAGEMENT

AI is undoubtedly making management more efficient by streamlining processes, analyzing data, and providing actionable insights. It optimizes workflows, predicts trends, and supports decision-making with incredible precision. However, AI's impact is primarily on management, which is distinct from leadership.

True LEAPership requires emotional intelligence, empathy, consciousness, awareness, and the ability to inspire and motivate people. LEAPers connect with their teams on a human level, fostering trust, collaboration, and a shared vision. This is irreplaceable.

LEAPers navigate complex interpersonal dynamics and provide the moral and ethical guidance that machines simply cannot replicate. AI lacks the capacity for genuine emotional engagement, creativity, and the nuanced understanding of human experiences that are crucial for effective leadership.

Therefore, while AI can enhance management functions, the essence of leadership remains a distinctly human quality that AI cannot replace.

USING THE LEAP PROCESS

At the outset of this book, I posed several questions: Are you prepared to lead in the age of AI? Can you harness the power of AI to LEAP to new heights? What does human intelligence look like in the age of artificial intelligence? How could we create a new paradigm of leadership to help us lead and leap in the age of AI?

I believe that the answers to these questions are embedded within the LEAP process—the approach to leadership that we have explored in this book, now considering the impacts of AI on leadership and vice versa. My intent has been to deepen the LEAP process through elevated thinking, decision-making, and strategies.

Throughout this book, I have used the LEAP process to expand strategies and thought processes, to question the status quo, and to bring to light issues that you may not have considered before. My goal has not been to provide definitive answers, but rather to give you a competitive edge over other leaders who are either too fearful of AI to engage with it or who are embracing it too much, ready to hand over all their control to it.

My ultimate aim has been to help you unleash your inner leader using the LEAP formula to achieve the results that you will need more than ever in the age of AI. As LEAPers, we have the potential to make a positive impact on the world in the face of uncertainty and adversity—as we are facing now. But to do so, we must continue to consciously elevate our human intelligence alongside the rise of artificial intelligence.

HARNESSING AI'S POWER FOR GOOD

While the age of AI encompasses both positive and negative aspects, as discussed throughout this book, our focus, as LEAPers, should always be on leveraging the positive. We must, of course, remain aware of the risks and the potential for negative consequences and results, but we need to work tirelessly to ensure we avoid those risks and reap the rewards. While influential figures such as Yuval Harari, and even Elon Musk and Bill Gates, have highlighted the potential risks of AI creating power imbalances and injustice, as LEAPers, we know that these concerns also present an opportunity to educate the public and build awareness in a way that advances us further, faster.

AI offers advanced strategies for accelerated learning, allowing us to become more efficient very quickly. By developing strategies of success centered around our unique skills, creativity, and passions, we can harness the power of AI to achieve greater things in the future. This is particularly true in that AI enhances our emotional intelligence and resilience, critical traits for navigating the modern world and the unknown landscape of the future. Cultivating a growth mindset is essential, where we focus on opportunities rather than obstacles and align our efforts with our desires. We can and must address these fears and uncertainties, but we cannot stay stuck in them.

Moreover, organizational culture and core values must evolve to set clear boundaries. Developing ethical guidelines and fostering diversity, equity, and inclusion (DEI) should be non-negotiable, with zero tolerance for misconduct. By integrating these principles, we can ensure that AI serves as a tool for positive change, empowering individuals and organizations to thrive ethically and sustainably in an AI-driven world. "AI must be used and operated by a leader who has a keen understanding and system in place for how to mitigate inherent AI biases and blind spots."[101]

A CALL TO ACTION FOR LEAPERS

As we look to the future of AI in leadership, several emerging trends, challenges, and opportunities come into focus clearly. The continuous evolution of AI will demand adaptive leadership styles that embrace flexibility and resilience. LEAPers must stay informed about technological advancements and cultivate a growth mindset to leverage AI's full potential. We must remain aware of this. We cannot let our foot off the pedal for even a moment. By fostering an environment that encourages ethical innovation, LEAPers can navigate the complexities of AI, driving positive outcomes for their organizations and society at large. We also cannot lose sight of the positive possibilities.

The bottom line is that AI is a powerful tool that can enhance our performance as leaders and shape the future across various fields. However, it can also dehumanize us and defraud us materially if unlawfully misused and psychologically affect our

---

[101] https://www.fastcompany.com/90938516/how-ai-can-make-us-better-leaders.

mental overwhelm, confidence, and well-being. Fortunately, this doesn't have to be the case if we follow the advanced LEAP process:

- L: Lean into Disruption
- E: Execute from a New Paradigm
- A: Align Wellness: Mind, Body, and AI
- P: Program Human Intelligence

By doing so, we can achieve a Quantum LEAP and embrace the future.

Ethical considerations will also remain of paramount importance in the context of AI in leadership. Issues related to privacy, bias, and accountability must be addressed to minimize inequalities and inherent biases that threaten AI and foster trust and transparency among our team. The development and adherence to ethical AI governance frameworks are essential to mitigate potential risks and ensure the responsible use of AI-powered tools.

AI's impact on leadership is a dynamic and evolving narrative. By reflecting on its rapid advancements, understanding its transformative potential, and addressing ethical implications, leaders can position themselves to harness AI's benefits while mitigating its risks. The future of AI in leadership holds immense promise, and with a thoughtful, responsible approach, leaders can ensure that AI serves as a powerful tool for enhancing human capabilities and driving progress.

As we stand on the brink of a new era defined by the rapid advancement of AI technology, the role of leadership is more critical than ever.

LEAPers, as we navigate the transformative era of AI, our leadership is paramount. We must adapt swiftly, embrace innovation, and explore the limitless potential of AI to drive organizational success. Yet, our responsibility extends beyond mere technological advancement. We must champion ethical practices, ensuring that AI is deployed fairly and equitably, free from the biases and injustices of the past.

Our actions have global ramifications, impacting gene manipulation, pollution, the economy, and societal well-being. As LEAPers, we adopt a global perspective, recognizing that our decisions shape not only our organizations but also the world we inhabit.

Let us forge ahead, driven by a deep understanding of AI's profound impact. Together, we can harness its power to create a future where technology serves humanity, empowering us to transcend our limits and build a better tomorrow.

To meet this call to action, LEAPers have the responsibility to shift their mindsets, recognizing that their decisions reverberate beyond local contexts, affecting communities worldwide. By integrating AI thoughtfully and strategically, leaders can make a positive impact, fostering sustainable practices and promoting economic growth while safeguarding our planet for future generations. The key element is to develop our human intelligence and leap beyond artificial intelligence.

LEAPING BEYOND AI

This book has provided a comprehensive road map for integrating AI into leadership, highlighting both the opportunities and challenges. In *Leap Beyond AI*, we explored how AI can enhance and transform leadership, enabling us to collaborate and innovate. We delved into the importance of maintaining a harmonious balance between digitization and our well-being, aligning our minds, bodies, and AI for optimal wellness. Furthermore, we emphasized the cultivation of human intelligence, recognizing its essential role in our human experience. Additionally, we ventured into uncharted territories of consciousness and sensing energy fields, harnessing their power to manifest our desires.

As we move forward, let us commit to leading with consciousness, intention, empathy, and integrity. Let us leverage AI to enhance our human intelligence, drive progress, and create a future where technology and humanity coexist harmoniously.

To *LEAP* beyond AI, we must, cultivate aspects of human intelligence that are integral to our human experience—unique qualities that drive our growth and evolution, including:

Consciousness—Human consciousness transcends mere data analysis and decision-making. It encompasses self-awareness, emotional depth, moral reasoning, and the ability to form personal connections and empathize with others. These qualities are deeply rooted in human experiences, interactions, and sensory perceptions, shaping our understanding of the world and ourselves. By forming personal connections with ourselves and others, we can foster a sense of interconnectedness and compassion that enriches our human experience and develops our consciousness.

Emotional Intelligence—While AI can be programmed to understand and empathize with human emotions, it lacks the conscious awareness and "aha moments" essential for truly experiencing emotions. AI cannot feel happiness, disappointment, joy, peace, freedom, responsibility, remorse, bliss, compassion, or unconditional love in the same way humans can.

Creativity—Human creativity is driven by emotions, experiences, and intuition, leading to novel solutions and self-expression. AI creativity relies on algorithms and data inputs, and AI excels in processing vast information. However, AI lacks emotional depth and the ability to create original ideas without human input. While AI can generate sophisticated outputs, it cannot replicate the abstract thinking and original concepts that arise from human creativity.

Intuition—Humans possess the unique ability to make decisions based on gut feelings, instincts, and subconscious cues, rather than relying solely on information. This intuitive sense, rooted in direct experiences of consciousness, is something AI cannot replicate. For instance, consider a person walking down a dark alley at night who suddenly feels a sense of danger or unease. Despite the absence of tangible evidence of a threat, their intuition, shaped by subconscious cues and past experiences, prompts them to swiftly change direction and avoid potential danger. This gut feeling serves as a powerful tool for survival and decision-making—a uniquely human trait that AI cannot mimic.

Morality and Ethics—AI functions based on algorithms and data, limiting its capacity to make independent moral judgments beyond what is programmed into it. For example, autonomous vehicles operate using algorithms to control actions like braking and changing lanes, but they may struggle with moral dilemmas such as choosing between harming occupants or pedestrians. This limitation highlights the ethical concerns of using AI for decision-making in complex scenarios.

Adaptability—Human adaptability encompasses cognitive flexibility, emotional intelligence, and cultural adjustments, enabling us to thrive in diverse environments. We adapt biologically, culturally, and technologically to our surroundings. On the other hand, AI adaptability relies on data processing and algorithmic adjustments, allowing for quick adaptation to new data inputs and tasks. However, it lacks the emotional and cultural contexts inherent in human adaptive processes. AI adaptability is limited by its programming and the data it receives.

Sensory and Sentient Experiences—While AI can analyze and describe sensations, it lacks the capacity to truly feel them. This limitation becomes apparent in music, where AI can identify patterns and structures but will never experience the emotional impact like a human listener. Human intelligence encompasses extrasensory perception. Humans have a unique capacity to sense and perceive subtle cues, emotions, and energies in a space that AI cannot replicate. Our inherent ability to connect with the world on a deeper, intuitive level allows us to pick up on nuances, emotions, and energies that AI may overlook or misinterpret.

Conscious Awareness—The ability of humans to engage in conscious awareness allows for personal growth, moral reasoning, and ethical decision-making based on values and principles. In contrast, AI operates based on programmed algorithms and data analysis, lacking the emotional depth and moral consciousness inherent in human intelligence. Thus, conscious awareness serves as a defining characteristic of human intelligence, enabling individuals to navigate the complexities of life, build meaningful relationships, and contribute to the collective evolution of humanity.

The question of whether AI will ever develop consciousness is a complex one, with no clear answer at this point in time. However, considering the rapid evolution of AI technology, it is not entirely implausible for AI to develop some aspects of consciousness and human qualities. As AI technology advances and researchers delve deeper into the realms of machine learning, neural networks, and cognitive computing, the possibility of AI developing some aspects of consciousness cannot be entirely dismissed. However, the complex nature of consciousness—with its subjective experiences, emotions, and self-reflection—poses significant challenges for replication in artificial systems.

By prioritizing these qualities in our leadership, we can ensure that AI is utilized in a manner consistent with our values and ethical standards. As the creators of AI, it is imperative that we possess a clear vision, purpose, and intention for our creation.

As we stand on the brink of a new era where AI can simulate so much of who we are, we must ask ourselves: what remains uniquely human? The answers may redefine our understanding of ourselves and our place in a rapidly evolving digital landscape.

As AI takes over daily (and often mundane) repetitive tasks, we're going to have more time to focus on what makes us truly human—our intelligence and creativity.

Think about it: we could dive into historical data to better understand how we've evolved, explore religious thinking in new ways, or even tackle massive issues like inequality and hunger. With AI handling the routine work, we could focus on solving the world's real struggles.

What is our true intention as humans in the development of AI? Is it to augment our own happiness and fulfillment, to propel progress and evolution as a species?

It is essential that we ponder these questions and ensure that AI aligns with our values and objectives. It is our responsibility to steer and mold the evolution of AI in a manner that is advantageous and congruent with our values as humans. In the era of artificial intelligence, true empowerment lies not in the technology itself, but in the conscious evolution of human intelligence.

This book serves as a reminder that while AI has the potential to revolutionize the way we work and live, it is ultimately up to us as leaders to guide its implementation in a way that benefits society as a whole. In the coming years, we must address the dangers posed by AI and implement necessary safeguards.

Undoubtedly, powerful technology in the hands of malicious actors presents significant risks.

In conclusion, the future of artificial intelligence holds immense potential for transforming society, industry, and daily life. From increased automation and personalized user experiences to advancements in healthcare and robotics, AI is poised to revolutionize how we live and work. As we navigate the ethical considerations and regulations surrounding AI, the collaboration between humans and machines will lead to enhanced decision-making and creativity. Ultimately, AI has the power to address global challenges and improve overall well-being, paving the way for a brighter and more innovative future.

As we stand on the cusp of this technological revolution, it is imperative that we prioritize the ethical and responsible development of AI systems. The potential risks, including the misuse of AI by bad actors or the unintended consequences of unregulated systems, cannot be ignored. It is essential that governments, organizations, and individuals work together to establish a framework that ensures AI is used for the benefit of humanity and not for destructive purposes.

The future of AI and its impact on society will be shaped by the decisions we make today. Let us not prioritize short-term gains over the long-term well-being of humanity. The regulation and control of AI must be a global priority, alongside other existential threats. Only by working together can we ensure that AI remains a force for good in our world.

Together, we can shape a future where AI is a powerful ally in our quest for a better world. We can rise to the challenge, embracing innovation and ethical leadership, and take bold steps toward a future where AI drives organizational success, global sustainability, and the human promise. The time for action is now. Let us lead the way.

Like you, I am well aware that by the time this book is published, there will be new technology, new apps, and new AI tools and platforms readily available. However, the underlying principles of this book are not based on what the latest innovation is, per se. Rather, they are about how to effectively use innovations, how to be more aware of the risks and opportunities, and how to reduce our fears, regardless of the specific problems.

Despite the chatter and fears surrounding AI, it will not replace leadership in the future. Instead, AI will enhance leadership. While AI technology continues to advance, it is true that qualities unique to human traits may be developed by AI. However, it is important to remember that AI is still a machine, no matter how advanced it becomes. It is, and always will be, a catalyst for leadership. The most important thing for leaders will be to remain aware and conscious of what comes next and how it will further refine leadership. It is up to us to redefine our leadership to allow us to LEAP beyond AI. The leaders who understand this and stay at the forefront of this evolution will reach new heights by tapping into opportunities that didn't exist before and navigate challenges confidently in our AI-driven, interconnected world.

As conscious leaders who seek meaning and impact, you face a pivotal decision—either adapt proactively or risk becoming obsolete. Opting to evolve empowers you to leverage the capabilities of AI, forge alliances with intelligent machines on your terms, and reshape the very essence of leadership in this ever-changing landscape. Embracing this approach will allow your leadership to thrive at the intersection of human intelligence and artificial intelligence.

Will we become disruptors or puppets?

The choice is, and always will be, ours.

What will you choose?

ABOUT THE AUTHOR

Micheline Nader, BSN, MPH, DESS is a renowned healthcare entrepreneur, best-selling author, Inspirational Leader, and change catalyst with a passion for personal development, leadership growth, and cultural transformation. With a background in healthcare management and entrepreneurship, Micheline has made significant contributions to the industry and beyond.

As the founder and CEO of Blue Dolphin Healthcare group, Micheline successfully built and managed a chain of skilled nursing homes in the Midwest before selling the company to a public healthcare group. Her entrepreneurial success is complemented by her role as President of Jesra Foundation Inc., a family foundation focused on education and health initiatives.

In addition to her entrepreneurial pursuits, Micheline is the author of two bestselling books, "Leap Beyond Success/ How

Leaders Evolve" and "The Dolphin's Dance," inspiring individuals and organizations to embrace personal growth and purposeful engagements.

Micheline holds a Bachelor of Science in Nursing (BSN) and a Master of Public Health (MPH) from the American University of Beirut, as well as a doctoral degree (DESS) in Healthcare Management from Paris-Dauphine University. She serves as a trustee of Fairleigh Dickinson University (FDU) and chairs the Board of Advisors at Silberman College of Business, while actively participating in various national boards and nonprofit organizations.

A visionary leader and influential figure, Micheline Nader is dedicated to making a positive impact on individuals and communities through her work, writing, and philanthropy. She has been recognized for her contributions with the Ellis Island Medal of Honor. "Leap Beyond AI" is her third book on leadership growth and development, showcasing her expertise and commitment to empowering others.

REFERENCES

1. Leap. (n.d.). Merriam-Webster.com Dictionary. https://www.merriam-webster.com/dictionary/leap

2. Jonze, S. (Director). (2013). Her [Motion picture]. Annapurna Pictures, Warner Bros. Pictures.

3. Built In. (n.d.). What Is Technological Singularity? Built In. https://builtin.com/artificial-intelligence/technological-singularity

4. Hern, A. (2014, February 22). Are the robots about to rise? Google's new director of engineering thinks so... The Guardian. https://www.theguardian.com/technology/2014/feb/22/robots-google-ray-kurzweil-terminator-singularity-artificial-intelligence

5. Research, A. I. M. (n.d.). When Will Singularity Happen? 1700 Expert Opinions of AGI (2024). https://research.aimultiple.com/artificial-general-intelligence-singularity-timing/

6. A Scientist Says the Singularity Will Happen by 2031. (2023, January 24). Popular Mechanics. https://www.popularmechanics.com/technology/a45780855/when-will-the-singularity-happen/

7. Built In. (n.d.). What Is Technological Singularity? Built In. https://builtin.com/artificial-intelligence/technological-singularity

8. A Scientist Says the Singularity Will Happen by 2031. (2023, January 24). Popular Mechanics. https://www. popularmechanics.com/technology/a45780855/when-will-the-singularity-happen/

9. ExpressVPN. (2023, February 6). What Is the AI Singularity? And When Will It Happen? ExpressVPN. https://www. expressvpn.com/blog/what-is-the-singularity-in-ai/

10. The AI Arms Race Could Enslave All of Us. (2018, September 14). YouTube. https://www.youtube.com/watch?v= Wn244ffkc8I

11. Mustafa Suleyman: AI Is Turning into Something Totally New. (n.d.). Reddit. https://www.reddit.com/r/singularity/ comments/1cafz4b/mustafa_suleymanai_is_turning_into _something/

12. Mo Gawdat: The Dangers of AI and How We Can Save Our Future. (2021, November 29). YesChat.ai. https://www.yes-chat.ai/blog-Mo-Gawdat-The-Dangers-Of-AI-And-How-We-Can-Save-Our-Future-37585)

13. Hern, A. (2014, February 22). Are the robots about to rise? Google's new director of engineering thinks so… The Guardian. https://www.theguardian.com/technology/2014/feb/22/ robots-google-ray-kurzweil-terminator-singularity-artificial-intelligence

14. ExpressVPN. (2023, February 6). What Is the AI Singularity? And When Will It Happen? ExpressVPN. https://www. expressvpn.com/blog/what-is-the-singularity-in-ai/

15. Research, A. I. M. (n.d.). When Will Singularity Happen? 1700 Expert Opinions of AGI (2024). https://research.aimul-tiple.com/artificial-general-intelligence-singularity-timing/

16. Built In. (n.d.). What Is Technological Singularity? Built In. https://builtin.com/artificialintelligence/technological-singularity

17. Research, A. I. M. (n.d.). When Will Singularity Happen? 1700 Expert Opinions of AGI (2024). https://research.aimultiple.com/artificial-general-intelligence-singularity-timing/

18. Built In. (n.d.). What Is Technological Singularity? Built In. https://builtin.com/artificialintelligence/technological-singularity

19. Research, A. I. M. (n.d.). When Will Singularity Happen? 1700 Expert Opinions of AGI (2024). https://research.aimultiple.com/artificial-general-intelligence-singularity-timing/

20. ExpressVPN. (2023, February 6). What Is the AI Singularity? And When Will It Happen? ExpressVPN. https://www.expressvpn.com/blog/what-is-the-singularity-in-ai/

21. Research, A. I. M. (n.d.). When Will Singularity Happen? 1700 Expert Opinions of AGI (2024). https://research.aimultiple.com/artificial-general-intelligence-singularity-timing/

22. Harris, S., & Yudkowsky, E. (2018, February 28). AI: Racing toward the brink. Intelligence.org. https://intelligence.org/2018/02/28/sam-harris-and-eliezer-yudkowsky/

23. Research, A. I. M. (n.d.). When Will Singularity Happen? 1700 Expert Opinions of AGI (2024). https://research.aimultiple.com/artificial-general-intelligence-singularity-timing/

24. Intelligence Community. (2021, March 16). Foreign Threats to the 2020 US Federal Elections. https://int.nyt.com/data/documenttools/2021-intelligence-community-election-interference-assessment/abd0346ebdd93e1e/full.pdf

25. Cahalan, S. (2022, November 17). The FBI Alleges TikTok Poses National Security Concerns. NPR. https://www.npr.org/2022/11/17/1137155540/fbi-tiktok-national-security-concerns-china

26. Fenton, C. (2023, September 6). AI to Replace 2.4 Million Jobs in the US by 2030, Many Fewer Than Other

Forms of Automation. The Register. https://www.theregister.
com/2023/09/06/generative_ai_jobs_forrester_report/

27. Ibid.

28. Fenton, C. (2023, September 6). AI to Replace 2.4 Million Jobs in the US by 2030, Many Fewer Than Other Forms of Automation. The Register. https://www.theregister.com/2023/09/06/generative_ai_jobs_forrester_report/

29. Ibid.

30. Recession and Automation Changes Our Future of Work, But There Are Jobs Coming, Report Says. (2020, October 22). World Economic Forum. https://www.weforum.org/press/2020/10/recession-and-automation-changes-our-future-of-work-but-there-are-jobs-comingreport-says-52c5162fce/

31. Misunderstanding and Misuse of Darwinism. (n.d.). Cambridge Core. https://www.cambridge.org/core/journals/european-review/article/abs/misunderstanding-and-misuse-of-darwinism/4C66214B7B70394A708FFA9DD49E9092

32. What Is Deepfake AI? A Definition from TechTarget. (n.d.). TechTarget. https://www.techtarget.com/whatis/definition/deepfake

33. Harnessing AI for Social Impact. (2022, December 8). Impact Entrepreneur. https://impactentrepreneur.com/harnessing-ai-for-social-impact/

34. Key Takeaways: AI for Social Innovation Report. (2020, October 29). MovingWorlds Blog. https://blog.movingworlds.org/ai-for-social-innovation-wef-report-summary/

35. 15 Impact Startups Using AI for Social Good. (2020, November 20). MovingWorlds Blog. https://blog.movingworlds.org/15-impact-startups-using-ai-for-social-good/

36. Key Takeaways: AI for Social Innovation Report. (2020, October 29). MovingWorlds Blog. https://blog.movingworlds.org/ai-for-social-innovation-wef-report-summary/

37. 6 Strategies for Using AI for Social-Emotional Learning. (2022, March 22). AI for Education. https://www.aiforeducation.io/blog/6-strategies-for-using-ai-for-social-emotional-learning; SEL + AI [Research Guide] – Social Emotional Learning - Inside SEL. (n.d.). Inside SEL. https://insidesel.com/sel-ai-research-guide/

38. SEL + AI [Research Guide] – Social Emotional Learning - Inside SEL. (n.d.). Inside SEL. https://insidesel.com/sel-ai-research-guide/; Artificial Intelligence and Social-Emotional Learning Are on a Collision Course. (2023, November 14). Education Week. https://www.edweek.org/leadership/artificial-intelligence-and-social-emotional-learning-are-on-a-collision-course/2023/11

39. 6 Strategies for Using AI for Social-Emotional Learning. (2022, March 22). AI for Education. https://www.aiforeducation.io/blog/6-strategies-for-using-ai-for-social-emotional-learning; SEL + AI [Research Guide] – Social Emotional Learning - Inside SEL. (n.d.). Inside SEL. https://insidesel.com/sel-ai-research-guide/

40. Artificial Intelligence and Social-Emotional Learning Are on a Collision Course. (2023, November 14). Education Week. https://www.edweek.org/leadership/artificial-intelligence-and-social-emotional-learning-are-on-a-collision-course/2023/11

41. 6 Strategies for Using AI for Social-Emotional Learning. (2022, March 22). AI for Education. https://www.aiforeducation.io/blog/6-strategies-for-using-ai-for-social-emotional-learning

42. Artificial Intelligence and Social-Emotional Learning Are on a Collision Course. (2023, November 14). Education Week. https://www.edweek.org/leadership/artificial-intelligence-and-social-emotional-learning-are-on-a-collision-course/2023/11

43. 6 Strategies for Using AI for Social-Emotional Learning. (2022, March 22). AI for Education. https://www.aiforeducation.io/blog/6-strategies-for-using-ai-for-social-emotional-learning

44. The Truth About Emotional Intelligence & AI: Thriving in an AI-Powered Era. (2023, January 18). LinkedIn. https://www.linkedin.com/pulse/truth-emotional-intelligence-ai-thriving-aipowered-d-reece-pcc; The Importance of Emotional Intelligence in the Age of AI - EI Design. (n.d.). EI Design. https://www.eidesign.net/emotional-intelligence-in-the-ai-age/

45. How AI Can Help You Develop Emotional Intelligence. (2023, March 24). Forbes. https://www.forbes.com/sites/forbescoachescouncil/2023/03/24/howai-can-help-you-develop-emotional-intelligence/

46. Ibid.

47. AI Is Fueling Our Obsession—and Humu Is the Key to People Evolution. (2023, August 10). Perceptyx. https://blog.perceptyx.com/ai-is-fueling-our-obsession-and-humu-is-the-key-to-people-evolution; Former Google Exec's Startup Humu Acquired. (2023, August 2). Forbes. https://www.forbes.com/sites/emmylucas/2023/08/02/former-google-execs-startup-humu-acquired-by-hr-platform-perceptyx/   H; Humu – Turn Strategy into Action. (n.d.). Humu. https://www.humu.com

48. Ibid.

49. Emotional Intelligence in AI | The Princeton Review. (n.d.). The Princeton Review. https://www.princetonreview.com/ai-education/emotional-intelligence-ai

50. The Importance of Emotional Intelligence in The Age of AI - EI Design. (n.d.). EI Design. https://www.eidesign.net/emotional-intelligence-in-the-ai-age/

51. Reece, D. (2023, January 18). The Truth About Emotional Intelligence & AI: Thriving in an AI-Powered Era. LinkedIn.

https://www.linkedin.com/pulse/truth-emotional-intelli-genceai-thriving-ai-powered-d-reece-pcc

52. Can AI Teach Us How to Become More Emotionally Intelligent? (2022, January 20). Harvard Business Review. https://hbr.org/2022/01/can-ai-teach-us-how-to-become-more-emotionally-intelligent

53. Emotional Intelligence in AI | The Princeton Review. (n.d.). The Princeton Review. https://www.princetonreview.com/ai-education/emotional-intelligence-ai

54. How AI Can Help You Develop Emotional Intelligence. (2023, March 24). Forbes. https://www.forbes.com/sites/forbescoachescouncil/2023/03/24/howai-can-help-you-develop-emotional-intelligence/

55. Ibid.

56. 10 Influential Voices in AI for Business & People Transformation. (2023, June 29). Lepaya. https://www.lepaya.com/blog/20-influential-voices-in-artificial-intelligence-forbusiness-people-transformation; Marr, B. (2019, November 25). The 10 Best Examples of How Companies Use Artificial Intelligence ... Bernard Marr & Co. https://bernardmarr.com/the-10-best-examples-of-how-companies-use-artificial-intelligence-in-practice/

57. Rehberg, E. (2023, July 3). How AI Is Transforming the Leadership Landscape in the 21st Century. Forbes. https://www.forbes.com/sites/forbescoachescouncil/2023/07/03/how-ai-is-transforming-the-leadership-landscape-in-the-21st-century/?sh=514508a467eb

58. The Surprising Reason Optimists Live Longer. (2022, February 24). Big Think. https://bigthink.com/neuropsych/optimism-and-longevity/

59. Hall, D. T. (2021). Leap Beyond Success. Amplify Publishing.

60. Career Insight: 5 Leadership Truths from Microsoft CEO Satya Nadella. (2022, August 10). Wharton Global Youth. https://globalyouth.wharton.upenn.edu/articles/career-insight/career-insight-5-leadership-truths-from-microsoft-ceo-satya-nadella/; From the Case Study on Satya Nadella (docx) - Course Sidekick. (n.d.). Course Sidekick. https://www.coursesidekick.com/management/13595860; Satya Nadella at Microsoft: Instilling a Growth Mindset. (2022, February 17). Publishing - London School of Business & Finance. https://publishing.london.edu/cases/satya-nadella-at-microsoft-instilling-a-growth-mindset/

61. Bercovici, A. (2023, October 20). How AI Can Help Leaders Make Better Decisions Under Pressure. Harvard Business Review. https://hbr.org/2023/10/how-ai-can-help-leadersmake-better-decisions-under-pressure

62. Maitra, A. (2023, March 2). How AI Can Make Us Better Leaders. Fast Company. https://www.fastcompany.com/90938516/how-ai-can-make-us-better-leaders

63. How AI Can Help Leaders Make Better Decisions Under Pressure. (2023, October 20). Harvard Business Review. https://hbr.org/2023/10/how-ai-can-help-leadersmake-better-decisions-under-pressure

64. The Importance of User-Centered Design in Product Development. (n.d.). StartMotion Media. https://www.startmotionmedia.com/the-importance-of-user-centered-design-in-product-development/

65. Center for Creative Leadership. (2023, March 22). A Leader's Best Bet: Exercise. https://www.ccl.org/articles/leading-effectively-articles/spotlight-on-exercise-andleadership/

66. Duncan, R. (2014, April 23). Fitness for Duty: Exercise Can Make You a Better Leader. Forbes. https://www.forbes.com

/sites/rodgerdeanduncan/2014/04/23/fitness-for-dutyexercise -can-make-you-a-better-leader/

67. What Role Does Nutrition Play in Good Leadership? (2022, June 21). Institute for Leadership. https://ilmovement.com/ blog/what-role-does-nutrition-play-in-good-leadership/

68. Center for Creative Leadership. (2023, March 16). 4 Components of Good Health and Effective Leadership. https://www. ccl.org/articles/leading-effectively-articles/4-components-good-health-enhance-leadership/

69. Ibid.

70. Ibid.

71. Ibid.

72. What Role Does Nutrition Play in Good Leadership? (2022, June 21). Institute for Leadership. https://ilmovement.com/ blog/what-role-does-nutrition-play-in-good-leadership/

73. Njawaya, S. (2023, January 18). Is Nutrition Important in Leadership? Fueling Performance & Smart Decision-Making. LinkedIn. https://www.linkedin.com/pulse/nutrition-impor-tant-leadership-fueling-performance-smart-njawaya-ap7lc

74. Ibid.

75. Maitra, A. (2023, March 2). How AI Can Make Us Better Leaders. Fast Company. https://www.fastcompany.com/90938516/ how-ai-can-make-us-better-leaders

76. Mark, G., & Voida, S. (2008). The Cost of Interrupted Work: More Speed and Stress. https://ics.uci.edu/~gmark/chi08-mark.pdf

77. Emotional Intelligence in Leadership. (n.d.). HBS Online. https://online.hbs.edu/blog/post/emotional-intelligence -in-leadership

78. Ibid.

79. Relationship Between Emotional Intelligence and Leadership. (n.d.). Korn Ferry. https://www.kornferry.com/insights/featured-topics/leadership/relationship-betweenemotional-intelligence-and-leadership

80. Ibid.

81. AI: Trust Survey 2023. (2023, March 8). Krista. https://krista.ai/ai-trust-survey-2023/

82. Ibid.

83. Ibid.

84. AI: Pattern Recognition Instead of Human Values. (n.d.). Central Michigan University. https://www.cmich.edu/news/details/ai-pattern-recognition-instead-of-human-values

85. Americans Spent $30.2 Billion Out-Of-Pocket On Complementary Health Approaches. (2012, December 12). National Center for Complementary and Integrative Health. https://www.nccih.nih.gov/news/press-releases/americans-spent-302-billion-outofpocket-on-complementary-health-approaches

86. Awakened Imagination and the Search. (n.d.). Awakened Imagination and the Search by Neville Goddard. https://www.awakenedimaginationandthesearch.org/tag/awakened-imaginationand-the-search-by-neville-goddard

87. The Power of Awareness. (n.d.). The Power of Awareness. https://www.thepowerofawareness.org/chapter-ten

88. The Power of the Subconscious Mind. (n.d.). Trend Culprit. https://trendculprit.com/power-of-the-subconscious-mind.pdf

89. The Inventor of Electroencephalography (EEG): Hans Berger (1873–1941). (2020, June 25). ResearchGate. https://www.researchgate.net/publication/339725586_The_inventor_of_electroencephalography_EEG_Hans_Berger_1873-1941

90. Quantum and Electromagnetic Fields in Our Universe and Brain. (2023, January 23). Frontiers. https://www.ncbi.nlm.nih.gov/pmc/articles/PMC8146693/

91. Ibid.

92. Quantum Manifestation: Co-Create a Life You Love with the Power. (n.d.). Ashley Melillo. https://www.ashleymelillo.com/blog/quantum-manifestation-creating-life-you-love

93. Ibid.

94. Finding Connections: Where Quantum Physics and Spirituality Meet. (2023, January 19). Lancaster Farming. https://www.lancasterfarming.com/country-life/family/finding-connectionswhere-quantum-physics-and-spirituality-meet/article_6a35965f-0cf2-594b-82e5-8d43b6e04d17.html

95. 8 Steps to Connect with the Universe and Create the Life You Want. (2021, February 26). Adam Hall. https://www.adam-hall.solutions/blog/2021/2/26/8-steps-to-connect-with-the-universeand-create-the-life-you-want

96. The Systems View of Life: A Unifying Vision. (2011). Cambridge Core. https://www.cambridge.org/core/books/systemsview-of-life/35186BA5B12161E469C4224B6076ADFE

97. Scharmer, C. O., & Kaufer, K. (2013). The Essentials of Theory U: Core Principles and Applications. Berrett-Koehler Publishers.

98. AI Agents Are the Next Frontier and Will Change Our Working Lives Forever. (2023, March 8). ZDNet. https://www.zdnet.com/article/ai-agents-are-the-next-frontier-and-will-changeour-working-lives-forever/

99. Ibid.

100. Generative AI in Organizations. (2023). Capgemini. https://www.capgemini.com/insights/research-library/generative-ai-in-organizations-2024/

101. How AI Can Make Us Better Leaders. (2023, March 13). Fast Company. https://www.fastcompany.com/90938516/how-ai-can-make-us-better-leaders

102. AI Readiness Assessment. (n.d.). Eide Bailly LLP. https://www.eidebailly.com/insights/tools/ai-readiness-assessment

103. Top 10 Business Applications of Artificial Intelligence. (n.d.). SC Training. https://training.safetyculture.com/blog/artificial-intelligence-business-applications/

104. 15 Top Applications of Artificial Intelligence in Business. (n.d.). TechTarget. https://www.techtarget.com/searchenterpriseai/tip/9-top-applications-of-artificial-intelligencein-business

105. Get Started on Your AI Journey with an AI Readiness Assessment. (n.d.). Baker Tilly. https://www.bakertilly.com/insights/getstarted-on-your-ai-journey-with-an-ai-readiness-assessment

106. Organization AI Readiness Assessment. (n.d.). Oxford Insights. https://oxfordinsights.com/ai-readiness/ai-readiness-selfassessment-tool-for-organisations/

MORE FROM MICHELINE NADER

FREE Tools

https://www.michelinenader.com/free-tools

LEAP Beyond AI Book Interaction:

Available and Upcoming Books by Micheline

https://www.michelinenader.com/books

LEAP Beyond AI Book Interaction:

Current and Upcoming Courses

https://www.michelinenader.com/courses/

LEAP Beyond AI Book Interaction:

CONTACT MICHELINE NADER

https://www.michelinenader.com/

LEAP Beyond AI Book Interaction:

LEAP Beyond Success Podcast:

https://www.michelinenader.com/podcast

SOCIAL MEDIA CONTACT INFO

- LinkedIn: https://www.linkedin.com/in/michelinenader/
- IG: https://www.instagram.com/michelinenaderofficial
- FB: https://www.facebook.com/michelinenaderofficial
- YouTube: https://www.youtube.com/@MichelineNaderOfficial
- TikTok:https://www.tiktok.com/@michelinenaderofficial
- X: https://x.com/MichelineKNader

Made in the USA
Middletown, DE
07 March 2025

72236385R00148